STITCH London

20 kooky ways to knit the city and more

Lauren O'Farrell

David and Charles

www.rucraft.co.uk

DEDICATION

For every Stitch Sage who has ever passed on the love of the knit at Stitch London. You're an inspiring bunch.

For Laura, Georgia, Grace, Sophie, Brigitte, Katie, Joelle, Candice, Emmy and Frances, the first cast-on row of Stitch London, who taught me the way of the knit.

And for lovely Sam, Prof. Lister, and all the staff of Bodley Scott at St Bartholomew's Hospital, without whom this knitter would not be knitting today.

NOTE

Keep all small items used in these projects, such as buttons and beads, out of reach of babies and young children.

A DAVID & CHARLES BOOK
© F&W Media International, LTD 2011

David & Charles is an imprint of F&W Media International, LTD
Brunel House, Forde Close, Newton Abbot, TQ12 4PU, UK

F&W Media International, LTD is a subsidiary of F+W Media Inc.
4700 East Galbraith Road, Cincinnati, OH 45236, USA

First published in the UK and USA in 2011

Text and designs © Lauren O'Farrell
Layout and photography © F&W Media International, LTD 2011

Lauren O'Farrell has asserted her right to be identified as author of this work in accordance with the Copyright, Designs and Patents Act, 1988.

The author and publisher have made every effort to ensure that all the instructions in the book are accurate and safe, and therefore cannot accept liability for any resulting injury, damage or loss to persons or property, however it may arise.

Names of manufacturers and other products are provided for the information of readers, with no intention to infringe copyright or trademarks.

A catalogue record for this book is available from the British Library.

ISBN-13: 978-0-7153-3867-4 paperback
ISBN-10: 0-7153-3867-6 paperback

Printed in China by Leo Paper Group
for F&W Media International, LTD
Brunel House, Forde Close, Newton Abbot, TQ12 4PU, UK

10 9 8 7 6 5 4 3 2 1

Publisher Alison Myer
Acquisitions Editors Jennifer Fox-Proverbs and Katy Denny
Desk Editor Jeni Hennah
Project Editor Nicola Hodgson
Senior Designer Mia Trenoweth
Photographers Sian Irvine and Jack Kirby
Senior Production Controller Kelly Smith

F+W Media Inc. publishes high-quality books on a wide range of subjects. For more great book ideas visit: www.rucraft.co.uk

Contents

Welcome to Stitch London

Stitch London isn't about being a master knitter with so much knitting knowledge rammed into your head that your eyes might pop out to reveal a perfectly stitched merino brain. It isn't about having yarn so fancy that you have to get your butler to knit it for you, or needles so shiny that they attract ravenous moths if you knit outdoors in summer. It's about loving to knit so much that you feel you may implode; putting your stitching stamp on everything in sight whether people like it or not (remember – you have pointy sticks if they don't), and surviving as a knitter in one of the world's most tangled and terrific cities.

Welcome to **Stitch London**.

London: city of puddled pavements, story-soaked streets, manky pigeons, sharp-elbowed commuters, jam-packed double-decker buses, shouty market sellers, bustling black cabs, vinegar-smelling chip shops, pubs packed with pint sippers, herds of camera-clicking tourists, and endless rivers of steaming hot tea.

Also a city of stitch-savvy knitters.

London knitters are everywhere. From the swish South Bank of the River Thames to the teetering tops of Tower Bridge, you are probably never more than ten metres away from a London knitter at any time. We have sticks, we have string and – little do non-knitters know – we are taking over the city.

In the midst of pointy spires, shiny skyscrapers, sloshy riversides and scurrying stitchers, *Stitch London* was born of the fact that I can't help but see London knitwise. And I'd like everyone else to see London knitwise, too.

THE SQUEE AND THE SWOON

Knitting should make you do one of two things: squee or swoon.

Swoony knits consist of floaty numbers made from wool sheared from sheep found only above the cloudline in deepest Peru's mystic mountains, where they're fed on silken grasses and drink only dew squeezed from the hair of beautiful maidens. They involve fancy stitches and complicated cast-ons. When you knit them, you need to be in a room with walls so thick that no sound can penetrate lest you lose your place in the pattern. When you hold up a finished swoony knit, people will go 'ahhhhhhh!' or 'ooooooo!'. They may pass out in the glorious radiance of your knit.

Squee knits are quite the opposite. They're sometimes made from cheap, squishy yarn in a garish shade you can't help loving. They're sometimes made of random leftover yarns, or yarn that is quite unsettling to buy, let alone knit with – eye-gouging colours, weird bobbly bits, and textures that

remind you of getting your teeth drilled. The stitches are simple but cleverly placed. When you knit them, people will ask you what on earth you're knitting; when you tell them, you'll get funny looks. When you brandish a finished squee knit, people will go 'squeeeeeeee!'; they will beam manically and may try to steal it. Don't let them! It's yours and they can't have it.

Stitch London is a squee knitting book. The patterns aren't fancy-schmancy, and they don't require you to be a sage of stitching. All you need is basic knitting knowledge, a willingness to switch on the part of your brain that has crazed ideas and let it run things for a while, and a total lack of yarn snobbery. Things might get fiddly, they might get funny, but I promise there will be squee.

THE CASTING ON OF DEADLY KNITSHADE

My Deadly Knitshade side, the part of me that appears like Dr Jekyll's Mr Hyde to knit up a storm when least expected, arrived when my first fledging stitches were cast on as a bit of a grrrr in the face of fate. I was six months into treatment for a rather pesky strain of cancer. Hodgkin's Lymphoma, a hungry type of blood cancer, had decided to take up residence in several bits of me and blow raspberries at medical attempts to evict it. Knitting was part of my attempt to wrestle myself back from the big C and get on with something slightly less scary.

Stitch London, the small group of stitchers I'd helped to create, arrived to sit and knit with me week after week. Those people, the stitching, and the worryingly large amount of cake we consumed, were a yarn-based distraction from other kinds of needles. I returned to Stitch London week after week, blood-test-bruised, occasionally bald, and bloody thrilled to be there.

I knitted (quite badly) in waiting rooms, on day wards while being filled with chemo (after ensuring my drip was placed so I could still stitch), in uncomfy hospital beds, at home after innard-crisping blasts of radiation, and eventually in yawnsome isolation after high-dose chemo and a bone marrow transplant that caused me to have to regrow my immune system from scratch. I may not have had any bone marrow, but I had two needles, some rather nice handpainted yarn and paltry, but oddly soothing, knitting skills.

Three years later, the evil cancer was vanquished, and it was quite clear that knitting (several nasty sets of chemo, stem-cell therapy, and numerous blasts of radiation aside) had totally cured me. It was a yarn-wrapped miracle. Woo hoo! Deadly Knitshade lived, she was much better at knitting, and she was consumed by the worrying ambition to conquer the world with her sticks and string.

Things were going to get woolly…

STITCH LONDON LIVES!

Stitch London (Stitch and Bitch London back then) hatched from a three-person egg of a knitting group (dreamt up by myself, Laura 'Purl Princess' Parkinson and Georgia 'Astrogirl' Reid, with the help of Debbie Stoller's *Stitch 'n Bitch* call to needles). We started off learning together. We loved it. We tempted others in.

Laura and Georgia moved on, but Stitch London had its claws in me. Escape was impossible. I now wrangle a roaring, city-stomping woolly Godzilla of thousands of stitchers. The group has taught hundreds of new knitters for free, and done marvellously mad knitting things. All because of one simple idea: knitting rules.

Knitting is addictive. After your first hit of knitting, you crave more. It's the kind of addiction you want other people to share, because you love it so all-consumingly. So much so that if knitting were a person, you'd have tattooed its name somewhere unmentionable, killed off all its exes and asked it to marry you by now. Knitting is the chocolate cake, the Johnny Depp, and the feel-good summer blockbuster of craft.

Teaching new knitters often makes me feel like a dodgy drug dealer lurking on a shadowy corner with yarn and needles. A fledgling Stitch Londoner arrives at a meeting with a shiny new pair of sticks, some untouched yarn and that wide-eyed baby-deer-in-the-headlights look. By the end of the evening, they're twitching with yarn greed; visions of smooshy socks and splendiferous shawls dancing behind their eyes.

This book encourages that 'you can cast on, but you'll never cast off' tradition. Here be patterns anyone can knit to drag you into the depths of knitting from which you will never escape. MWA HA HAAAA!

THE SCARY WORLD OF PATTERN MUTATIONS

Those two needles in your hands (or four needles if you're a DPN-er) are your electricity-conducting attachments. That humble ball of yarn is the lifeless body of your monster. You, the simple knitter, are Dr Frankenstitch, and it is up to you to bring every pattern to life.

There are people who won't bungee jump in case they end up as a puddle of jam on the pavement. There are people who won't try Stilton because it smells like feet. And, sadly, there are people who won't step off the beaten track of a pattern and make it their own. To those people, I make chicken noises and shake my head despairingly.

A knitting pattern is a mere suggestion of what you'll end up with. In this book, I encourage you to totally mess with my patterns. Grab them by the stitches, twist them, shake them, turn them purple, love them, hug them and call them George. When you cast on your knitting, it is just that – *your* knitting. Throw in a few stitches here, a new colour there, extra arms, a section of unexpected rib, a set of teeth, marmalade, a bit of fairisle or, gasp, a row or two of ugly eyelash yarn. Mix buttons, pipe cleaners, watch cogs, cat hair, glitter glue, beads, and all manner of crafty bits together with your knitting and see how they get on. They might have beautiful babies, or you might produce something that you later have to drag down to the Thames and drown. It might be traumatic, but at least you can say that you and your knitting lived.

All Aboard: Exploring **Stitch London**

Stitch London can be explored any way you choose. Stroll firmly through from start to finish like an industrious City worker; buzz about alighting on patterns you take a fancy to in the style of a Hyde Park bumble bee, or stumble from section to section in a random order like an after-hours West End night clubber searching for that elusive night bus home.

This section is a friendly helping hand to help you navigate your way along the pavements of **Stitch London** patterns, so you can knit without any niggles. The rest is up to you and your trusty needles. Happy travels, and mind the gap.

DIFFICULTY RATINGS

To help you find your way through the patterns in *Stitch London*, we've rated the projects with difficulty levels – with a little London twist.

There are similarities between how you get around London and how you get around a knitting pattern. You're either a new knitter, fresh off the plane, all wide-eyed and a little lost; a clued-up knitter, strutting the streets with the confidence of an Oyster card-carrying, umbrella-wielding local; or a stitch sage, roaring down back roads and nipping up side streets like a home-grown London cabbie.

Tourist – Patterns for newbie knitters who stick to the tube map and don't wander into unknown territory.

London Local – For knitters who know their way around a stitch, but sometimes need to check their *A–Z*.

Black Cab Driver – Projects for dyed-in-the-wool knitters with 'The Knowledge' of all things knitty in the city.

GUBBINS

'Gubbins' means stuff and things. In this book, it means the materials that you'll need to make each project: yarn, needles and all the other bits.

ALL CHANGE

These sections shove you gently in the direction of making your knit your own. Never feel that you have to stick rigidly to a pattern: the whole point of your knitting is that it's yours and no one else's. So make something that has bits of your brain all over it. Not the actual gooey stuff inside your head, but the ideas that grow in that goo. Treat your needles as your paintbrush and the yarn as your paint. Pour the weird workings of your imagination on them and watch what grows.

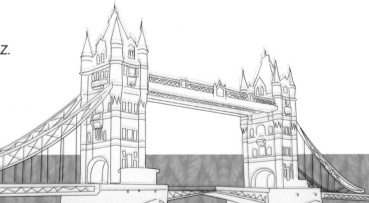

ABBREVIATIONS

Ahhhh. A little gaggle of knitting abbreviations. So sweet, all tucked into the pattern in neat little rows. Abbreviations are the bits of a knitting pattern that resemble complicated algebraic equations. They're the bits that make non-knitters peering over your shoulder turn slightly green and need a sit down. They're also the bit that Dumbledore loves the best in the *Harry Potter* books. Lucky for you, they're easy-peasy. Roll your eyeballs over this lot and feel free to come back if you forget any.

approx. – approximately
beg – beginning
cm – centimetre(s)
DK – double knitting
DPN – double-pointed needle
g – gram(s)
in – inch(es)
inc – increase(s)/increasing
inc1 – increase one; knit into front and back of stitch to increase
k – knit
k2tog – knit two stitches together (decrease by one stitch)
k3tog – knit three stitches together (decrease by two stitches)
ktbl – knit through the back loop
m – metre(s)
m1 – make one; increase using stitch lying between two stitches
mm – millimetre(s)
oz – ounces
p – purl

p2tog – purl two together (decrease by one stitch)
psso – pass slipped stitch over
rem – remain/ing
rep – repeat
skp – slip 1, knit 1, pass slipped stitch over (decrease by one stitch)
sl – slip
ssk – slip, slip, knit; slip two stitches one at a time, knit two slipped stitches together (one stitch decreased)
st(s) – stitch(es)
st st – stocking stitch (US: stockinette stitch)
tbl – through back of loop
tog – together
yd – yards(s)
* – repeat directions following * as many times as indicated or to end of row
( ) – repeat instructions in round brackets the number of times indicated

LONDON LINGO

Londoners have their own language, built on the foundation of the Queen's BBC English and then chewed up and spat out on the gritty city streets by cab drivers, market-stall shouters, and ruddy-faced pub landlords. If you want to Stitch London, you have to learn a little of the lingo or you'll be lost. Here are a few words to help you find your way:
battenburg – the pink and yellow king of cakes. Wrapped in a marzipan jacket of sugary goodness.
berk – a rather foolish individual.
blinder – an excellent thing or achievement. Woo hoo! 'This fairisle jumper was a proper blinder.'

bog-standard – plain and ordinary 'The newbie bought bog-standard metal knitting needles to begin with.'
bovver – aggressive, thuggish behaviour.
faffing – messing around and wasting time. Tut.
gammy – see **manky**.
gubbins – stuff and things. In this book, it means the materials you'll need to make each project.
manky – diseased and a bit disgusting. Yuck.
me old mucker – my friend. How nice.
mince pies – 'eyes' in cockney rhyming slang.
newbie – brand-new, shiny-eyed knitter. Awwww.

not really cricket – not a very nice thing to do. Shame on you.
Oyster card – ticket for all manner of London transport. Not a card for shellfish.
skint – penniless or poor.
throw a wobbly – have a huge, dramatic tantrum.
toerag – scallywag, scoundrel, imp.
tube – London's underground transport system. Full of sweaty commuters.
wellies – rubber boots made for jumping in puddles. Splosh.
WIP – Work in Progress. Your knit while it is being knit.
'You're nicked!' – you are under arrest.

STITCH ESSENTIAL GUBBINS

Before you embark on your journey through the streets of *Stitch London*, you will need to arm yourself with some wool-wrangling weapons. Here's a list of stuff you won't survive without.

Knitting needles
Straight needles
These fellows are long, straight and pointy in metal, plastic or wood. You are not going to get far without these, so pick ones you like the feel of. You're going to be holding them a lot.

Circular needles
These guys are two needles joined together with a cord. Good for knitting tubes, knitting on the tube (they're shorter so are less intrusive when elbow room is tight) or for the wonder of the magic loop (see The Way of the Knit).

DPNs
They wander in sets or four or five and are used for circular knitting. Also seem to scare or fascinate fellow commuters if you break them out while travelling.

Gubbins case
A case in which you stash all the fiddly bits you need when knitting. Pencil cases work well, as do glasses cases, tins, make-up bags or boa constrictors (it can be hard to get the stuff back out of a snake, though).

Darning/tapestry needle
A big fat needle for weaving in ends and sewing up. Get a few, as you will lose some to the hungry Tapestry Needle-Eating Monster that stalks us all.

Sewing needle
The fiddly cousins of tapestry needles. These bad boys are ultra-pointy. Be careful where you leave them when not using them.

Scissors
Get good, small portable ones that fit in your gubbins case. There will be chopping galore.

Tape measure
In the case of most knits, size does matter. A retractable tape measure is the way to go. If it's shaped like a sheep or a cake, even better.

Thread
Always useful for a million things; you can have various colours to hand, but black and white are essential.

Stitch markers
These little rings mark places in your knitting so you don't get lost. So kind. You can buy them or just make them from spare yarn. I use tiny elastic bands for braids.

Crochet hook
This little hook is your 999 emergency aid if you drop a stitch. Use it to pick the stitch back up and fix it. It's also the queen of making long lines of lovely chain stitch.

Small notebook and pen
Scribble down rows, pattern changes, or hilarious doodles of your boss being eaten by a dragon.

Project bag
Your WIP (Work in Progress) is going to need a home when it's not in your hands. If you shove it in your bag and get lip balm all over it or find it's taken a shine to your sunglasses and refuses to be parted from them, well, you'll be sorry. Get a simple drawstring bag, bung it in a plastic bag, or stuff it in a disused sock you stole from a giant.

Stuffing
Forget fancy craft-shop stuffing. Butcher an old pillow or a bargain-shop cushion. Their outsides may be grotty, but their precious innards can be reused.

Beads, buttons and shiny stuff
We're all magpies at heart. Start stashing embellishments where you find them. Snip buttons off holey garments bound for the bin, hoard beads from broken bling, and keep your eyes out for bargains.

Eyes
If you only have eyes for the ones you love, you're going to have lots of unfinished WIPs. Bag yourself some safety eyes and seed beads to bring your knits to starey life.

Felt
You can make anything from felt. Anything at all. Honest. If you can't be faffed to knit extra bits, felt works almost as well. Not that I'm suggesting you use felt for everything. But, when in doubt, felt.

Wire and/or pipe cleaners
Pipe cleaners and wires give knits their very own skeletons. A bendy knit is a happy knit; just make sure no eyes are poked out by unruly ends. Tuck them in well.

NON-ESSENTIAL GUBBINS

Stitch holder
This doohickey is to put stitches on that you're not working for a little while, so you can get on with knitting the others. You can also thread them on a spare bit of yarn if you're a bit skint.

Claw clips
Those little crocodile claw clips you use for holding up long hair are perfect for holding together a seam while you sew it. Get some.

Tweezers
Fiddly crafting, such as stuffing tiny knits or threading beads, is made a thousand times easier with tweezers. Plus you can pluck that unsightly nose hair, too.

Pliers
A pointy pair of craft pliers is good for poking, bending and pulling. Also good for doing crocodile impressions.

Row counter
You click it or roll it each time you complete a row. It remembers it all for you, allowing you to wander off and dream about much more important things such as how much yarn you can fit in the cupboard under the stairs without your family noticing.

Pins
For stretching out and blocking knits. For voodoo. For cleaning under your nails.

KNITTING TRANSLATIONS

English on this side of the pond in Blighty and on the other side of the pond in the US isn't quite the same. Autumn is fall, pavements are sidewalks, and jam is jelly. We Brits like our words for things to have no connection with their meaning whatsoever. Americans say what they mean.

In knitting there are some differences too. Here's a bit of help if you are lost in translation.

UK term	US term
4ply yarn	sport-weight yarn
cast off	bind off
DK (double knitting) yarn	worsted-weight yarn
double moss stitch	moss stitch
moss stitch	seed stitch
stocking stitch	stockinette stitch
tension	gauge

UK AND US NEEDLE AND HOOK SIZES

Needles, the sticks of your stitching, come in different sizes for different-sized stitches. Just to make things doubly confusing, the UK and Europe label their sizes differently from the US. Brits and Europeans keep things neatly metric; Americans prefer to throw a nice round number in there. Not all sizes have a direct equivalent in the US, either. You can name them yourself if you like. I'll call that one Horace.

Knitting needle sizes

Metric	US
2mm	0
2.25mm	1
2.5mm	–
2.75mm	2
3mm	–
3.25mm	3
3.5mm	4
3.75mm	5
4mm	6
4.5mm	7
5mm	8
5.5mm	9
6mm	10
6.5mm	10½
7mm	–
7.5mm	–
8mm	11
9mm	13
10mm	15
12mm	17

Crochet hook sizes

Metric	US
2.25mm	B1
2.5mm	–
2.75mm	C2
3mm	–
3.25mm	D3
3.5mm	E4
3.75mm	F5
4mm	G6
4.5mm	7
5mm	H8
5.5mm	I9
6mm	J10
6.5mm	K10½
8mm	L11
9mm	M/N13
10mm	N/P15
12mm	O16

YARN

There is no such thing as the right yarn. The patterns in this book show colour and size of yarn. This gives you an idea of what kind of yarn you need without loudly insisting you use a particular yarn and nothing else. Your yarn is entirely up to you. For those who must create an exact replica or they'll implode, there's a list of some of the yarns used at the back of the book (see Suppliers). However, some projects were made from shocking label-less yarn, which I either found in the depths of my stash pile or bought from a cart pulled by a haughty Indian cow in the muggy streets of the desert city of Jaisalmer. That would be a long way to go to get the right yarn.

UK yarn weights	US yarn weights
2ply	super fine weight
4ply	sport weight
DK	worsted
aran	medium weight
chunky	bulky weight
super chunky	super bulky
Godzilla chunky*	Godzilla bulky*

*Please note: Godzilla-sized yarn is purely fictional. Such a shame.

"Little London Landmarks

This little phone box liked his pudding.

London has building bits that are dripping with history. The landmarks may have stony faces, but underneath they're bursting with tales to tell. Tottering past them with your camera and guidebook, you can spy hundreds of years of London's stories built into their bricks and mortar.

Make yourself some Little London Landmarks by stitching a **Baby Big Ben**, a **Tiny Tower Bridge** and a **Pint-sized Parliament Telephone Box**. Employ bits of the city as bookends, doorstops, letter racks or terribly fancy pincushions. Then, if you make enough bits of the city, you can stomp about them roaring in radioactive Godzilla style. RAAAAARRRGHHHH!

Yarn o'clock and all is quiet...

BABY BIG BEN

BONG! BONG! BONG! Big Ben is the giant bell that dwells in St Stephen's Tower. It's as Londony as it gets when it comes to London landmarks, and you can stitch your own with the greatest of ease. It should really be called Small St Stephen's Tower. Baby Big Ben is wrong, but lovely to say out loud.

Unlike the real clock tower, there won't be many tourists peering up at this one snapping photos – unless you're desperate for your Baby Big Ben to feel giant, in which case put it on a very high shelf and invite camera-toting tourists into your house.

GUBBINS

Needles
Pair of 4mm (US size 6) needles

Yarn
25g (⅞oz) light browny-yellow DK (worsted) for tower walls
15g (½oz) dark grey DK (worsted) for roof
Small amount of any colour DK (worsted) for area under Big Ben
15g (½oz) gold DK (worsted) for clock area

Other bits
Stuffing
Heavy filling to stabilize base of tower (steel shot, sand, tiny pebbles, baking beans or, if you're really rich, gemstones)
Felt for sewing cube-shaped container for heavy filling
4 wooden clock face buttons or ordinary buttons with clock faces drawn on
Thick cardboard or foam for shaping sides

Difficulty: London Local
Size: Approx. 25cm (10in) high
Gauge: 20 sts and 30 rows = 10cm (4in) in pattern

PATTERN

Sides of Tower (make 4)

Cast on 11 sts in light browny-yellow yarn.

Row 1 P, k to last st, p.

Row 2 K, p to last st, k.

Rows 3–16 Rep row 1 (odd) and 2 (even).

Row 17 P across.

Row 18 K, p to last st, k.

Row 19 P across.

Rows 20–26 Beg row 2 rep row 1 (odd rows) and 2 (even rows).

Row 27 P across.

Row 28 K, p to last st, k.

Row 29 P across.

Rows 30–36 Beg row 2 rep row 1 (odd rows) and 2 (even rows).

Row 37 P across.

Row 38 K, p to last st, k.

Row 39 P across.

Rows 40–46 Beg row 2 rep row 1 (odd rows) and 2 (even rows).

Row 47 P across.

Row 48 K2, *p, k, rep three times from *, p, k2.

Row 49 P2, *k, p, rep three times from *, k, p2.

Row 50 K across.

Row 51 P2, k7, p2.

Row 52 K2, p7, k2.

Rows 53–58 Beg row 51 rep row 51 (odd rows) and 52 (even rows).

Row 59 P across.

Row 60 K2, *p, k, rep three times from *, p, k2.

Row 61 P2, *k, p rep three times from *, k, p2.

Row 62 K across.

Change colour to dark grey yarn for roof.

Row 63 P across.

Row 64 P across.

Row 65 K2tog, knit to last 2 sts, k2tog (9 sts).

Row 66 P across.

Row 67 K across.

Row 68 P2tog, p to last 2 sts, p2tog (7 sts).

Row 69 K across.

Row 70 P across.

Row 71 K2tog, k to last 2 sts, k2tog (5 sts).

Row 72 P across.

Row 73 K across.

Row 74 P across.

Row 75 K across.

Row 76 P2tog, k, p2tog (3 sts).

Row 77 K3tog.

Thread yarn through st.

Polymer clay makes good clock face buttons if you can't get your paws on buttons like the lovely carved wooden ones I used. Poke holes in where the ends of the hands should be and sew through them to show the time.

Clock Areas (make 4)

Cast on 10 sts in gold yarn.

K 10 rows.

Cast off (bind off).

Area under Big Ben

Cast on 11 sts in any colour yarn.

Work 10 rows st st.

Cast off (bind off).

FINISHING

Sew all four sides together, from roof to bottom of tower.
Stuff top of tower.
Cut four 12 × 5.5cm (4¾ × 2¼ in) rectangles of cardboard or foam.
Place inside to hold up Big Ben.
Stuff, leaving 5cm (2in) at bottom.
Cut felt to make a 5cm (2in) cube.
Sew felt into a cube, leaving top open.
Fill cube with heavy filling and sew top closed. Place cube carefully in bottom of tower.
Sew Area under Big Ben onto bottom of tower to secure cube.
Sew gold clock areas on to each face of tower.
Embroider tip of tower with gold yarn.
Sew on clock face buttons.

ALL CHANGE
Baby Big Ben has a basic skyscraper shape. A little silver and fewer purled ledges could turn it into Canary Wharf, one of your own city's church towers, or general bits of cityscape.

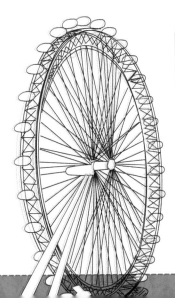

TINY TOWER BRIDGE

The first test of proving yourself a real Londoner is not confusing Tower Bridge with nearby London Bridge. London Bridge is the one you can see Tower Bridge from. Tower Bridge is the one with the towers. London's Tower Bridge was born in 1886 and is impressively made of 70,000 tons of concrete and 1,100 tons of steel. Tiny Tower Bridge won't use quite that much in materials. It will, however, be just as impressive. Honest, guvnor.

GUBBINS

Needles
Pair of 4mm (US size 6) needles

Yarn
50g (1¾oz) light browny-yellow DK (worsted) for tower walls
25g (⅞oz) dark grey DK (worsted) for roof
Small amount of light blue DK (worsted) for walkways and bridges
Small amount of white DK (worsted) for embellishing walkways

Other bits
Stuffing
Heavy filling to stabilize bases of towers
Felt for sewing envelope container for heavy filling
Silver embroidery thread
Gold embroidery thread
Thick cardboard or foam for shaping sides

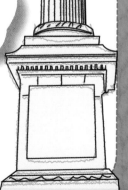

Difficulty rating: Black Cab Driver
Size: Approx. 22cm (8½in) high
Gauge: 20 sts and 30 rows = 10cm (4in) in pattern

PATTERN NOTES

You'll need to make two Towers to create each end of the bridge. Each Tower consists of Front, Back, two Sides and one Under Bridge. There are two Walkways and two Bridge bits to join them up.

You are going to grumble at how many very similar bits of this you have to knit. Sorry about that.

PATTERN

Fronts and Backs of Towers

Left Leg (make 4)
Cast on 5 sts in light browny-yellow yarn.
Row 1 P, k3, p (5 sts).
Row 2 K, p3, k.
Rows 3–10 Rep row 1 (odd rows) and 2 (even rows).
Row 11 Inc1 twice, k2, p (7 sts).
Row 12 K, p across.
Row 13 Inc1 twice, k4, p (9 sts).
Row 14 K, p across.
Leave sts on needle.

Right Leg (make 4)
Cast on 5 sts in light browny-yellow yarn.
Row 1 P, k3, p (5 sts).
Row 2 K, p3, k.
Rows 3–10 Rep row 1 (odd) and 2 (even).
Row 11 P, k2, inc1 twice (7 sts).
Row 12 P to last st, k.

Row 13 P, k4, inc1 twice (9 sts).
Row 14 P to last st, k.
Leave sts on needle.

Knit bits of this in public and then weird people out by telling them you're knitting Tower Bridge when they ask.

Front (make 2)
Starting with Right Leg, knit across both legs to join them.
Row 15 P, k across to last st, p (18 sts).
Row 16 K, p across to last st, k.
Row 17 P across.
Row 18 K, p to last st, k.
Row 19 P across.
Rows 20–26 Beg row 16 rep row 15 (odd rows) and 16 (even rows).
Row 27 P across.
Row 28 K, p to last st, k.

Row 29 P across.
Rows 30–36 Beg row 16 rep row 15 (odd rows) and 16 (even rows).
Row 37 P across.
Row 38 K, p to last st, k.
Row 39 P across.
Rows 40–46 Beg row 16 rep row 15 (odd rows) and 16 (even rows).
Row 47 P across.
Row 48 K across.

Change colour to dark grey yarn for roof.

Row 49 P across.
Row 50 P across.
Row 51 K2tog, knit to last 2 sts, k2tog (16 sts).
Row 52 P across.
Row 53 K2tog, knit to last 2 sts, k2tog (14 sts).
Row 54 P across.
Row 55 K2tog, knit to last 2 sts, k2tog (12 sts).

Row 56 P across.
Row 57 K2tog, knit to last 2 sts, k2tog (10 sts).
Row 58 P across.
Row 59 K2tog, knit to last 2 sts, k2tog (8 sts).
Row 60 P across.
Row 61 K2tog, knit to last 2 sts, k2tog (6 sts).
Row 62 P across.
Row 63 K2tog, k2, k2tog (4 sts).
Row 64 P across.
Row 65 K2tog twice (2 sts).
Thread yarn through sts.

> Place small, energetic pet rodents on your tiny monument and pretend that they're oversized sewer rats freed from London's underbelly and hungry for the city's supply of cheese.

Back (make 2)
Rep instructions for Front.

Tower Sides (make 4)
Cast on 11 sts in light browny-yellow yarn.
Row 1 P, k to last st, p.
Row 2 K, p to last st, k.
Rows 3–16 Rep row 1 (odd) and 2 (even).
Row 17 P across.
Row 18 K, p to last st, k.
Row 19 P across.
Rows 20–26 Beg row 2 rep row 1 (odd rows) and 2 (even rows).
Row 27 P across.
Row 28 K, p to last st, k.
Row 29 P across.
Rows 30–36 Beg row 2 rep row 1 (odd rows) and 2 (even rows).
Row 37 P across.
Row 38 K, p to last st, k.
Row 39 P across.
Rows 40–46 Beg row 2 rep row 1 (odd rows) and 2 (even rows).
Row 47 P across.
Row 48 K across.

Change colour to dark grey yarn for roof.

Row 49 P across.
Row 50 P across.
Row 51 K2tog, knit to last 2 sts, k2tog (9 sts).
Row 52 P across.
Row 53 K across.
Row 54 P2tog, purl to last 2 sts, p2tog (7 sts).
Row 55 K across.
Row 56 P across.
Row 57 K2tog, k to last 2 sts, k2tog (5 sts).

Row 58 P across.
Row 59 K across.
Row 60 P2tog, p, p2tog (3 sts).
Row 61 K across.
Row 62 P across.
Row 63 K2tog, k (2 sts).
Row 64 P2.
Row 65 K2tog (1 st).

Thread yarn through st.

Under Bridge (make 2)
Cast on 11 sts in light blue yarn.
Rows 1–35 Work in st st starting with k row.
Cast off (bind off) all sts.

'envelopes' 4.5cm (1¾in) high and sew, leaving top open. Fill envelopes with heavy filling and sew tops closed. Place envelopes carefully in the bottom of each leg of the tower between the cardboard and the inside of the legs.

Freak out your postman by ordering your heavy filling via mail order, then muttering while you sign for it that the tiny, oddly heavy, parcel is plutonium and that you are an evil genius bent on taking over the world.

Stuff each tower. Try to keep them as square as possible. It's easier to form the stuffing into a squarish shape before you put it in.

Bridge and Walkways (make 4)
Cast on 3 sts in light blue yarn.
Rows 1–40 K across.
Cast off (bind off).

Gold and silver embroidery thread make everything classy. You will want to embroider everything in sight once you start. Have self-control or you'll end up overblinging. No one likes an overblinger. Less is more.

FINISHING

Sew together long edges of front, back and sides of each tower.
Sew together two sides of roof, leaving the other two open.
Sew Under Bridge across bottom of each tower. The short edge goes along the tower side and the longer edge across bottoms of front and back of tower in a curve.
Cut four 12 x 5.5cm (4¾ x 2¼ in) rectangles of cardboard. Place cardboard inside each tower to hold up the sides.
Cut felt to make four 11 x 6.5cm (4½ x 2½in) rectangles. Fold rectangles into

The smaller your heavy filling, the more important it is to make sure your felt filling envelope is leak-free. Get a plastic bag involved if you're worried about leakage, especially with sand or grit. A knit leaving a trail of grit is not cool.

Sew up roof.

Using silver embroidery thread, sew windows onto each tower. There are lots of windows. Have patience. It will be worth it. If you're lazy, you can cut out felt windows or glue on material instead.

Sew 'X' pattern across both walkways using white yarn.

Sew the ends of both walkways between the towers under the top 'ledge'.

Sew the ends of both bridges between the towers under the bottom 'ledge'.

Embroider a little point of gold on top of each tower.

Stare about you in wonder at all the yarn ends, bits of felt, scraps of embroidery thread and piles of stuffing you seem to have amassed.

Tidy it all up. Keep everything for other projects. Yarn ends make fabulous stuffing.

Go and make a cup of tea.

Sit back and admire the Tiny Tower Bridge you have just created.

ALL CHANGE

The basic bits of Tower Bridge can be used to create loads of other landmarks. It's all in the easy rectangles and a little bit of simple embroidery. Create bits of your own city, from your humble home to the hallowed halls of churches or shiny sticks of skyscrapers.

PINT-SIZED PARLIAMENT TELEPHONE BOX

GUBBINS

Needles
Pair of 4mm (US size 6) needles
2.5mm (US B1/C2) crochet hook

Yarn
30g (1oz) red DK (worsted) for telephone box sides and top
Small amount of white DK (worsted) for telephone sign
10g (⅓oz) any colour DK (worsted) for base
15g (½oz) silver 4ply (sport) for windows

Other bits
Stuffing
Heavy filling to stabilize base of telephone box
Felt for sewing cube-shaped container for heavy filling
White felt for telephone sign (optional)
Black embroidery thread
Thick cardboard or foam for shaping sides

Pah to your mobile phone! It has nothing on the scarlet sentinel that is the London phone box. This red devil has been offering Londoners use of the 'dog and bone' since 1924, as well as providing a place for Busty Babs of Bethnal Green and Voluptuous Vera of Vauxhall to adorn with calling cards to advertise their dubious talents. In the shadow of Big Ben, within cigar-smoke-smelling distance of the Winston Churchill statue, sits London's most photographed phone box, in protester-plagued Parliament Square. Stitch yourself a woolly version of this cheeky crimson chap.

Difficulty rating: London Local
Size: Approx. 12cm (4¾in) high
Gauge: 17 sts and 28 rows = 10 cm (4in) in pattern

PATTERN

Phone Box Sides (make 4)

Cast on 14 sts in red yarn.
Work 22 rows in st st (k odd rows, p even).
Row 23 P across.
Row 24 P, change to white yarn, p to last st, change to red, p.
Row 25 K, change to white yarn, k to last st, change to red, k.
Row 26 Rep row 24.
Rows 27–29 K across in red.
Row 30 P2tog, p10, p2tog (12 sts).
Row 31 K2tog, k8, k2tog (10 sts).
Row 32 P2tog, p6, p2tog (8 sts).
Row 33 K2tog, k4, k2tog (6 sts).
Row 34 P2tog, p2, p2tog (4 sts).
Cast off (bind off).

Phone Box Top

Cast on 12 sts in red yarn.
Work 14 rows in st st.
Cast off (bind off).

Phone Box Base

Cast on 14 sts in any colour yarn.
Work 15 rows in st st.
Cast off (bind off).

Windows (make 3)

Cast on 15 sts in silver yarn.
Work 20 rows in st st.
Cast off (bind off).

Long Window Strips (make 6)

Using 2.5mm (US B1/C2) crochet hook chain 15 sts in red yarn.

Short Window Strips (make 15)

Using 2.5mm (US B1/C2) crochet hook chain 12 sts in red yarn.

FINISHING

Sew all four sides together.
Sew top onto four sides.
Cut four 8 x 10cm (3¼ x 4in) rectangles of cardboard or foam.
Place inside to hold up phone box.

Stuff, leaving space 5.5cm (2¼in) deep at bottom.

Cut felt to make a cube 5.5cm (2¼in) on all sides.

Sew felt into a cube shape, leaving top open.

Fill cube with heavy filling and sew top closed.

Place the filled cube carefully in the bottom of the phone box.

Sew the base of the phone box closed to secure the cube.

Sew windows to three sides of the phone box.

Sew the window strips across the windows, two long strips vertically and five short strips horizontally.

Using black thread, embroider the word 'Telephone' on the white panels on all four sides.

If the knit is too loose to embroider then cut felt rectangles to size, embroider and sew in place.

Amuse yourself by sewing an unsuspecting friend's mobile phone into the phone box. Phone them and watch their brain slowly melt as they realize you've gone to the length of handsewing their phone into a tiny woollen replica of a London phone box. Best to try this on friends who either have a good sense of humour or who you don't like very much and don't mind losing.

ALL CHANGE

If you're a Dalek-fighting Gallifreyan at hearts (excuse the terrible Dr Who in-joke) you might want to knit the Phone Box in dark blue and turn it into the Tardis. I can't help you make it bigger on the inside than the outside, though.

Go crazy with odd bits of your yarn stash and recreate Knit the City's Phone Box Cosy in tribute to one of London's most daring sneaky stitching triumphs (see www.knitthecity.com).

"Little Londoners

There are a whole lot of people in London. Now you can knit some of them. Or, if you're feeling ambitious, you can knit all of them. But at the time of writing there are 7,556,900 people living in London, so you'd best start now.

Meeting London's locals is all part of getting hopelessly lost in and falling in love with the city of pubs and pigeons. May I introduce you to a band of Little Londoners who help keep the city ticking over? Say hello to **Queen Liz**, who broke out the yarn and needles to knit for the soldiers during World War Two (she's one of us knitters, crown or no crown), with her stitched security to keep an eye on her.

Now one can stitch a little sovereign of one's own, with a couple of **Queen's Guards** and some purled **Police** to keep those pesky paparazzi at bay.

THE QUEEN

Visit London and you can't escape from the Queen. No, I'm not implying that she randomly stalks citizens like some kind of royal ninja, but you can see Lizzie gazing out serenely from our pounds and pennies, giving it some vogue on our stamps, and bestowing the royal wave from more Queen-themed shiny souvenir goodies than you can shake a sceptre at.

You can stand this knitted Queen as a stately sentry by your finest English Breakfast tea caddy; dangle her from your Christmas tree in time for the Queen's festive speech; or send her as a stately souvenir to someone who thinks all things royal are awfully quaint.

GUBBINS

Needles
Set of four 3.5mm (US size 4) double-pointed needles or circular needle for magic loop (see The Way of the Knit)
2.25mm (US B1) crochet hook

Yarn
10g (⅓oz) light pink DK (worsted) for skin
10g (⅓oz) purple/royal blue DK (worsted) for dress and crown
Small amount of red DK (worsted) for cloak
Small amount of white DK (worsted) for cloak and crown trim
Small amount of yellow DK (worsted) for crown
Small amount of brown or grey DK (worsted) for hair

Other bits
Stuffing
Shiny fake gems (or real ones if you're rich) to decorate the crown
Beads for eyes
Clear 'peel and stick' glue
Cling film (plastic wrap) or plastic bag
Felt for feet (optional)
Cardboard for base (optional)

Difficulty rating: Black Cab Driver
Size: Approx. 9cm (3½in) high
Gauge: Not important

PATTERN

Head and Body

Cast on 3 sts on one DPN in light pink yarn.
Push sts to other end of needle.
Row 1 Inc1 3 times as I-cord (see The Way of the Knit) (6 sts).
Row 2 Join and knit around, arranging 2 sts on each of three DPNs.
Round 3 Inc1, inc1 each needle (12 sts).
Round 4 K.
Round 5 K3, inc1 each needle (15 sts).
Round 6 K.
Round 7 K.
Round 8 K4, inc1 each needle (18 sts).
Round 9 K.
Round 10 K4, k2tog each needle (15 sts).
Round 11 K.
Round 12 K3, k2tog each needle (12 sts).
Round 13 K.

Stuff the head.

Round 14 K2, k2tog each needle (9 sts).
Round 15 K.
Round 16 K1, k2tog each needle (6 sts).

Change to purple/royal blue yarn.

Round 17 K.
Round 18 Inc1, inc1 each needle (12 sts).
Round 19 K.
Round 20 K3, inc1 each needle (15 sts).
Round 21 K.
Round 22 K4, inc1 each needle (18 sts).
Rounds 23–32 K.
Round 33 Inc1 each st (36 sts).
Round 34 K.

Stuff the body.

Cut yarn with 10cm (4in) tail, thread yarn through all stitches, pull tight and knot. To flatten the base, you can insert a circle of cardboard about 2.5cm (1in) across before you tighten the stitches (optional).

Arms

Cast on 3 sts on one DPN in purple/royal blue yarn.
Push sts to other end of needle.
Knit 10 rows as I-cord.
Change to light pink yarn.
Knit 3 rows as I-cord.
Pull yarn through sts and knot.
Rep for second arm.

> This pattern is unashamedly fiddly. No one said making people would be easy-peasy. Just ask Dr Frankenstein.

Crown

Bowl of crown

Cast on 12 sts in purple/royal blue yarn.
Knit 6 rows in st st.
Row 7 K2tog across (6 sts).
Cut 10cm (4in) tail, thread yarn through sts and pull tight.
Turn purl-side out and sew short edges together to make a 'bowl'.
Turn knit-side out.

Gold bits of crown

Using 2.25mm (US B1) crochet hook chain 15 sts in yellow yarn.
Cut 10cm (4in) tail, thread yarn through st.
Use tails to sew ends of gold bits to four sides of bowl and top to form a cross.

Trim of crown

Cast on 2 sts in white yarn.
Push sts to other end of needle.
Knit 20 rows as I-cord.
Cut 10cm (4in) tail, thread yarn through sts.
Sew trim around bottom of bowl to complete crown.

> Weave in your ends properly. The Unravelling Fairy is merciless in her attacks on lazy end-weavers.

Cloak

Main part of cloak

Cast on 15 sts in red yarn.
Knit 15 rows.
Row 16 P2tog, p11, p2tog (13 sts).
Row 17 K.
Row 18 P2tog, p9, p2tog (11 sts).
Row 19 K.
Row 20 P2tog, p7, p2tog (9 sts).
Row 21 K.
Row 22 P2tog, p5, p2tog (7 sts).
Cast off (bind off).

Collar and bottom trim of cloak

Cast on 2 sts in white yarn.
Push sts to other end of needle.
Knit 10 rows (for collar) or 20 rows
(for bottom trim) as I-cord.
Cut 10cm (4in) tail, thread yarn
through sts.

Side trims of cloak

Using 2.25mm (US B1) crochet
hook chain 18 sts in white yarn.
Cut 10cm (4in) tail, thread yarn
through st.
Rep for second trim.

Hair (by Amy MacPherson)

Cut 20 3cm (1¼in) strands of brown
or grey yarn.
Place some cling film (plastic wrap) or
part of a plastic bag onto the head of
your Queen and cover the scalp area
in glue.
Lay the plastic on a flat surface.
Starting at the edges and working to
the centre, place the yarn ends onto
the glue area to make circles of loops
all pointing outwards.
Wait for the glue to dry and then peel
away the scalp (or cut around the scalp
shape, depending on what glue you
used). You should have a flexible head
of hair.

When you've made a wig for
a Little Londoner test it out
by putting it on your cat to
see how it looks. Cats love
dressing up. Fact.

FINISHING

Sew arms either side of body.
Sew collar and trims to cloak and sew
cloak around neck.
Cut two felt rectangles with rounded
ends for feet (optional).
Stick fake gems on crown and sew
crown to top of head.
Sew on beads for eyes.
Practise curtsey in front of Queen.

ALL CHANGE

This Queen is the young and funky model. You can make the
more mature Queen by adding silvery-grey hair and HUGE
speech-reading glasses for authenticity.

And what kind of a Queen Liz would she be without her
faithful corgis? You can stitch her tiny snuffling hounds, too.
Just make sure to walk them twice a day. They may have little
legs, but they still need exercise. See www.knitthepigeon.com
for the pattern.

THE QUEEN'S GUARD

The Queen's Guards aren't meant to move apart from at the Changing of the Guard, even if you go up to them and prod them with a 9mm bamboo needle. Although I wouldn't recommend trying that…

The Guards also get to wear bearskin hats. I suggest you leave the bears out of this and make your hat with fuzzy yarn.

GUBBINS

Needles
Set of four 3.5mm (US size 4) double-pointed needles or circular needle for magic loop (see The Way of the Knit
2.25mm (US B1) crochet hook

Yarn
10g (⅓oz) skin colour DK (worsted) for head and hands
10g (⅓oz) red DK (worsted) for tunic
Small amount of black fuzzy (eyelash) yarn for bearskin hat
Small amount of black DK (worsted) for collar and trousers
Small amount of white DK (worsted) for belt
Small amount of yellow/gold DK (worsted) for chin strap

Other bits
Stuffing
Beads for eyes
Felt for feet (optional)
Cardboard for base (optional)

Difficulty rating: Black Cab Driver
Size: Approx. 9cm (3½in) high
Gauge: Not important

PATTERN

Head and Body

Cast on 3 sts on one DPN in skin colour yarn.
Push sts to other end of needle.
Row 1 Inc1 3 times as I-cord (see The Way of the Knit) (6 sts).
Row 2 Join and knit around, arranging 2 sts on each of three DPNs.
Round 3 Inc1, inc1 each needle (12 sts).
Round 4 K.
Round 5 K3, inc1 each needle (15 sts).
Round 6 K.
Round 7 K.
Round 8 K4, inc1 each needle (18 sts).
Round 9 K.
Round 10 K4, k2tog each needle (15 sts).
Round 11 K.
Round 12 K3, k2tog each needle (12 sts).
Round 13 K.

Stuff the head.

Round 14 K2, k2tog each needle (9 sts).
Round 15 K.
Round 16 K1, k2tog each needle (6 sts).

Change to black yarn.
Round 17 K.
Round 18 Inc1, inc1 each needle (12 sts).

Change to red yarn.
Round 19 K.
Round 20 K3, inc1 each needle (15 sts).
Round 21 K.
Round 22 K4, inc1 each needle (18 sts).
Rounds 23–27 K.

Change to black yarn.
Rounds 28–32 K.
Round 33 Inc1 each st (36 sts).
Round 34 K.

Stuff the body.

Cut yarn with 10cm (4in) tail, thread yarn through all stitches, pull tight and knot.
To flatten the base, you can insert a circle of cardboard about 2.5cm (1in) across before you tighten the stitches (optional).

Arms
Cast on 3 sts on one DPN in red yarn.
Push sts to other end of needle.
Knit 10 rows as I-cord.

Change to skin colour yarn.
Knit 3 rows as I-cord.
Pull yarn through sts and knot.
Rep for second arm.

Belt

Using 2.25mm (US B1) crochet hook chain 20 sts in white yarn.
Cut 10cm (4in) tail, thread yarn through st.

Bearskin Cap

Fuzzy part of cap

Cast on 15 sts using fuzzy black yarn.
Knit 18 rows.
Cut 10cm (4in) yarn, pass yarn through sts and pull tight.
Use yarn to sew up long edges to form cap.

Chin strap of cap

Crochet chain of 15 sts in yellow/gold yarn.
Cut 10cm (4in) tail, thread yarn through st.

FINISHING

Sew arms either side of body.
Use yellow/gold yarn to embroider buttons on the red tunic and black collar.
Sew belt around waist of Guard and sew on chin strap and hat. Embroider buckle of belt in yellow/gold yarn.
Sew on beads for eyes.
Cut two rounded black felt rectangles for feet (optional).
Make enough guards so that you can ceremoniously change them at intervals.

The Queen's Guard's gun is made with the magic of a cotton bud, the end of a cable tie, black permanent marker and some glue. Just don't tell him that.

THE POLICE

Bobbies, Peelers, The Fuzz, The Filth, Coppers, The Old Bill, Bow Street Runners or the Boys and Girls in Blue. Call them what you will, London's police force are a handy verbal A–Z, an amused but disapproving eye when you're hanging precariously off the neck of a Trafalgar Square lion, and a slap on the wrist for the city's wrongdoers.

While you knit a woolly bringer of the law you can practise lines such as 'You're nicked, mah son!' and 'You're goin' dahn tahn, ya toerag!' to add some East London authenticity.

GUBBINS

Needles
Set of four 3.5mm (US size 4) double-pointed needles or circular needle for magic loop (see The Way of the Knit)
2.25mm (US B1) crochet hook

Yarn
10g (⅓oz) skin colour DK (worsted) for head and hands
Small amount of hair colour DK (worsted) for hair
15g (½oz) dark blue DK (worsted) for jacket, trousers and hat
Small amount of black DK (worsted) for belt
Small amount of grey/silver DK (worsted) for buttons, buckle and hat

Other bits
Stuffing
Beads for eyes
Clear 'peel and stick' glue
Cling film (plastic wrap) or plastic bag
Felt for feet (optional)
Cardboard for base (optional)

Difficulty rating: Black Cab Driver
Size: Approx. 9cm (3½in) high
Gauge: Not important

PATTERN

Head and Body

Cast on 3 sts on one DPN in skin colour yarn.

Push sts to other end of needle.

Row 1 Inc1 3 times as I-cord (see The Way of the Knit) (6 sts).

Row 2 Join and knit around, arranging 2 sts on each of three DPNs.

Round 3 Inc1, inc1 each needle (12 sts).

Round 4 K.

Round 5 K3, inc1 each needle (15 sts).

Round 6 K.

Round 7 K.

Round 8 K4, inc1 each needle (18 sts).

Round 9 K.

Round 10 K4, k2tog each needle (15 sts).

Round 11 K.

Round 12 K3, k2tog each needle (12 sts).

Round 13 K.

Stuff the head.

Round 14 K2, k2tog each needle (9 sts).

Round 15 K.

Round 16 K1, k2tog each needle (6 sts).

Change to dark blue yarn.

Round 17 K.

Round 18 Inc1, inc1 each needle (12 sts).

Round 19 K.

Round 20 K3, inc1 each needle (15 sts).

Round 21 K.

Round 22 K4, inc1 each needle (18 sts).

Rounds 23–32 K.

Round 33 Inc1 each st (36 sts).

Round 34 K.

Stuff the body.

Cut yarn with 10cm (4in) tail, thread yarn through all stitches, pull tight and knot.

To flatten the base, you can insert a circle of cardboard about 2.5cm (1in) across before you tighten the stitches (optional).

Put your tapestry needle back where you found it or it'll disappear off to the Home for Abandoned Tapestry Needles. A sad, sad place.

Arms

Cast on 3 sts on one DPN in dark blue yarn.

Push sts to other end of needle.

Knit 10 rows as I-cord.

Change to skin colour yarn.

Knit 3 rows as I-cord.

Pull yarn through sts and knot.

Rep for second arm.

Belt

Using 2.25mm (US B1) crochet hook chain 20 sts in black yarn.

Cut 10cm (4in) tail, thread yarn through st.

Hat (Policewoman)

Cast on 15 sts in dark blue yarn.

Row 1 K.

Row 2 P.

Row 3 * K, k2tog, rep five times from * (10 sts).

Rows 4–6 Work in st st starting with a purl row.

Row 7 K2tog across (5 sts).

Cut 10cm (4in) of yarn, thread yarn through sts.

Turn purl-side out and sew up short

sides to make hat.
Turn knit-side out.
Allow brim to roll up.

Hat (Policeman)
Cast on 15 sts in dark blue yarn.
Row 1 K.
Row 2 * P, p2tog, rep five times from *
(10 sts).
Rows 3–9 Work in st st starting with
a purl row.
Row 10 K2tog across (5 sts).
Finish as for Policewoman's hat,
without brim.

Hair
Cut 20 strands of yarn in hair colour
and length you want.
Put cling film (plastic wrap) onto the
head of your Little Londoner and cover
scalp area in glue.
Lay plastic on flat surface.
Starting at the edges and working
to the centre, place one end of each
strand onto glue to make the wig
(make loops if you want curly hair),
all pointing outwards or away from
the 'parting'.
Wait for glue to dry and then peel
away scalp (or cut around scalp shape,
depending on the glue you used).
You should have a flexible head of hair.

FINISHING

Sew arms either side of body.
Sew belt round waist. Use silver yarn to
embroider buttons, belt, buckle and hat.
Add hair, and frayed strand of yarn for
policeman's moustache.
Sew on beads for eyes.
Cut two rounded black felt rectangles
for feet (optional).

ALL CHANGE
You've made one purled person, you've made them all. Use the Head, Body and
Arms patterns and then mix and match the hair, hats and accessories to make
whoever you fancy. Knit your nan, purl your postman, handmake Harry Potter,
cast off Winston Churchill or stitch up Shakespeare. Knit yourself an entire
army of monkey butlers to do your bidding while you sit and knit. Go on!

Rat Race
London

"Going Underground"

London's commuters are as mad as a box of frogs. Angry, sweaty, sleepy frogs who need their coffee and would sell their granny for a seat on the train. The city in rush hour is a faceless stampeding herd of elbows, umbrellas, bags, books, mobile phones and take-away coffee cups, whose urgent cry of 'CAN YOU MOVE DOWN INSIDE THE CARRIAGE, PLEASE!' can be heard echoing through the underground.

If you're going to survive the daily city swarm, you're going to need to toughen up. Learn the steely your-bag-does-not-need-a-seat-of-its-own glare and perfect the there-is-room-for-one-more-and-that-one-is-me push for train embarkation. You'll also need to tool up with some commuter kit essentials: touch in with your ticket-toting **Tubeline Scarf**, expand your mind while you're squished like a sardine with your **Commuter Book Cosy**, and stand out from the stampede with your **Bag Bovver**. Arrive at your destination rested, well read and covered in knit. Mind the doors, please.

No one suspects I'm reading 'Twilight'

The scarf rocked the Oyster card to sleep...

TUBELINE SCARF

Under London, in the guts of the city, lurks the London Underground, or 'The Tube', as those of us who shoot about in its belly call it. The city gulps down whole herds of Londoners; worm-like tubes squirm through the tunnels and then rudely belch travellers out into the cloudy sunlight. The Tubeline Scarf celebrates this subterranean sojourn in a rush of stripes. It proudly parades 12 tube-map colours: gregarious green for the District, mellow yellow for the Circle, broody black for the Northern, tarty turquoise for the Waterloo and City, moody magenta for the Metropolitan, perky pink for the Hammersmith and City, smooth silver for the Jubilee, rowdy red for the Central, devious dark blue for the Piccadilly, optimistic orange for the inside-out Overground, lively light blue for the Victoria, and bustling brown for the Bakerloo. The scarf also features a sneaky ticket pocket to slip your Oyster card into (or your work pass, or microfilm with international conspiracy details). Wrap yourself up warmly, slap your card on the reader and sashay through in one smooth movement like a true Londoner.

GUBBINS

Needles
4mm 40cm-long circular needle (US size 6, 16in long)

Yarn
50g (1¾oz) DK (worsted) yarn in 12 colours (suggested colours below, but use whatever you like):
Green for District Line
Yellow for Circle Line
Black for Northern Line
Turquoise for Waterloo and City Line
Purple/magenta for Metropolitan Line
Pink for Hammersmith and City Line
Silver/grey for Jubilee Line
Red for Central Line
Dark blue for Piccadilly Line
Orange for Overground
Light blue for Victoria Line
Brown for Bakerloo Line

Other bits
Stitch marker
2 × popper buttons for pocket
Crochet hook (any convenient size) for making tassels
15cm (6in) square piece of cardboard for making tassels

Difficulty rating: Tourist
Size: 10 x 160cm (4 x 63in)
Gauge: 24 sts and 30 rows = 10cm (4in) in st st

PATTERN NOTES

The Tubeline Scarf is knitted in 12 colours in this order: green, yellow, black, turquoise, purple/magenta, pink, silver/grey, red, dark blue, orange, light blue and brown.

PATTERN

Scarf

Cast on 50 sts in green yarn.
Row 1 K across.
Place marker at start of row and join to knit in the round.
Rounds 2–20 K around.

> Weave in the ends as you go. Having some kind of yarn-end squid once you're finished can be a bit disheartening.

Change to next colour.
Round 21 K around.
Round 22 Sl1, k around.
Rounds 23–40 K around.

Rep rounds 21–40 with each colour twice, ending on a second brown stripe. Cast off (bind off).

> If someone asks what you're knitting while you're on the tube, tell them you're knitting the entire London Underground. You can twitch a bit too if you like. Might get you a bit of elbow room.

Ticket Pocket

Cast on 20 sts in colour of your choice.
K 24 rows.
Cast off (bind off).

FINISHING

Sew up cast-off (bound-off) end of scarf to close end. Leave the other end open to help you sew on the pocket. Sew three sides of the ticket pocket square onto the first yellow stripe of the scarf.

> While your scarf is open at one end, you can slip it onto the cat to make a very long hat. Trust me; the cat will love it.

Sew on two small popper buttons to fasten the top of the pocket.
Sew up the cast-on end of the scarf.
Sigh loudly as you think you've finished. Realize to your horror that you still need to make the tassels.

Tassels

Mark places for 6 tassels with scrap yarn at each end of the scarf (just pull a bit through; there's no need to knot it).

Don't spend too long trying to work out tassel colour combos. It will make your brain hurt.

Cut a 15cm (6in) square of cardboard to wrap yarn around.
Taking one colour at a time, wrap 6 strands of yarn around cardboard.
Cut yarn loops at the bottom to make 6 x 30cm (12in) strands.
Repeat for each colour so you have 72 strands.

Put a magnet into the ticket pocket of your scarf and you could stick it on the fridge when you get home. Why you'd want to do this is beyond me.

Take all strands of one colour and fold in half into a loop.
Using a crochet hook, pull about 5cm (2in) of the end of loop through end of scarf at first marker.
Take cut ends and pass them through the loop.
Pull the tassel tight.
Repeat with each colour for each of the marked tassel spots.

Repeat all for the other end of the scarf. Go on.

Whip your scarf around your neck and Snoopy dance around the room in triumph. That was a whole lot of knitting.

Attempt to confuse ticket inspectors by waving your scarf at them in a hypnotic manner when they ask for your ticket. But do buy a ticket. I'm not suggesting you fare-dodge.

ALL CHANGE

The colourful tangle of London's tube map isn't your only choice. Unearth tube maps from your favourite cities and transform your Tubeline Scarf into a travelling token. Give it some 'Zut alors!' with the 14 colours of the Paris Metro. Keep it maple-syrup-soaked Canadian with the four colours of Montreal's Metro, eh? Knit a scarf that never sleeps with the Noo Yoik Subway's ten colours. Make it Muscovite with the 12 colourski of the Moscow Metro. Stitch up a bonza beaut with the 11 colours of Sydney's City Rail. Or make it 'semplice e bella' with Rome's two shades.

COMMUTER BOOK COSY

A book's cover says volumes about you to your fellow sardine-tin-squashed travellers. Make sure yours says something nice by showing off your stitching and keeping your hard-working book comfy with the Commuter Book Cosy. When it's your stop, button it up, hook your finger through the fastener, and get going. Your book will thank you and that nosy bloke across the aisle won't have a clue what you're reading either. Ha!

GUBBINS

Needles
4.5mm (US size 7) needles
3.5mm (US E4) crochet hook

Yarn
50g (1¾oz) of any colour DK (worsted) for book cosy
Small amount of any colour DK (worsted) for fastener
Small amount of any colour DK (worsted) for bookmark

Other bits
Stitch markers (or bits of scrap yarn)
Three buttons
Stuff to embellish your book cosy with (embroidery thread, felt, beads, sequins, fabric, shark's teeth, eye of newt, toe of frog; you get the idea…)

Difficulty rating: Tourist
Size: Approx. 14 x 21cm (5½ x 8¼in) folded. Will fit most paperbacks and a fair few hardback ones. Add or take away a few stitches for weirder-sized books.
Gauge: 16 sts and 24 rows = 10cm (4in) in st st

PATTERN

Book Cosy

Book Cosy Flap

Cast on 34 sts.

Row 1 K2, * p2, k2, rep eight times from *.

Row 2 P2, * k2, p2, rep eight times from *.

Rows 3–10 Rep row 1 (odd rows) and row 2 (even rows).

Row 11 K across.

Row 12 K3, p28, k3.

Rows 13–22 Rep row 11 (odd rows) and row 12 (even rows).

Book Cosy Cover

Mark start of cover with stitch marker.

Rep rows 11 (odd rows) and 12 (even rows) until piece measures 28cm (11in) from marker.

Mark end of cover with stitch marker.

Book Cosy other Flap

Row 1 K across.

Row 2 K3, p28, k3.

Rows 3–12 Rep row 1 (odd rows) and row 2 (even rows).

Row 13 K2, * p2, k2, rep eight times from *.

Row 14 P2, * k2, p2, rep eight times from *.

Rows 15–22 Rep row 13 (odd rows) and row 14 (even rows).

Cast off (bind off) loosely in pattern.

> Your cover doesn't need to look like the actual cover of the book. Take the bits of the book you love and use them wisely.

Fastener

Cast on 7 sts holding two strands of yarn together.

Row 1 K, p, k, p, k, p, k.

Rows 2–40 Rep row 1.

Cast off (bind off) in pattern.

Using 3.5mm (US E4) crochet hook chain 10 sts to make loop.

Bookmark

Using 3.5mm (US E4) crochet hook chain 36 sts.

Cut 3 6cm (2½in) strands of yarn.

Fold in half and use crochet hook to pull 3 loop ends through last st of chain. Pass other ends through loop and pull tight to make tassel.

Sew the Bookmark to the top of the Book Cosy in the middle.

FINISHING

Make flaps: fold each end inward at the points where the markers have been placed and then sew the top and bottom together.

Sew 5cm (2in) of one end of Fastener to the middle of the outside edge of the back cover. Make sure it is stitched in strongly. Sew the crocheted loop to the other end of the Fastener.

Sew three buttons to the front of the Book Cosy 3cm, 6cm and 9cm (1¼in, 2½in and 3½in) from the edge.

Snuggle your book into the cosy and button it up. If you listen closely, you may hear your book purr. A cosy book is a happy book…

> Buttons are king. Keep your eye out for good ones. Although stealing them off people's clothes while distracting them with bad magic tricks is not really cricket.

ALL CHANGE

The humble book cosy can be very easily adapted. Make a dark and dusty detective novel; a sugar-coated summer read; or a moss stitch (US: seed stitch), rune-embroidered elvish fable. Take any pattern or stitch style and use it in the cover part of your book cosy. Just remember to check that your gauge isn't wildly different first.

And why stop at books? Get your needles into a celebratory Greeting Card Cosy. If you're going to say it, say it with yarn. See www.knitthepigeon.com for pattern.

Felt rules over fiddly intarsia and embroidery. Hunt down a shape that works (an internet search, a bit of paper and some screen-tracing magic saves printing); cut it out, use the template to chop it out of the felt and blanket stitch.

From top left, clockwise:
Monster Book: Furry yarn, safety eyes, toggles and the feeling the book may bite you.
His Dark Materials: Felt, blanket stitch, snow buttons, dæmons and armoured bears.
Penguin Classic: Stripes and flightless bird buttons.
Howl's Moving Castle: Felt, beads, silver sparkle yarn, falling stars and fire demons.
Mortal Engines: Chinese coins, broken watches, strong glue and cities on wheels.
Harry Potter: Felt, blanket stitch, brass buttons, lightning scars and a seeker's skills.

BAG BOVVER

GUBBINS

Needles
Pair of 5.5mm (US size 9) needles

Yarn
Acrylic DK (worsted) yarn in colours of your choice

Other bits
Up to you (buttons, beads, embroidery thread, jam, dinosaur bones, etc)
Strips of sew-on Velcro (hook side only) long enough to line edges of area you want to cover

You've got your phone, knitting, wallet, book, Swiss Army knife with handy fish scaler and wood saw, spare knitting in case you finish the first knitting, emergency chocolate ration, knitting pattern, Ravelry name badge, headphones, MP3 player, knitting bits, camera, anti-zombie spray in case of apocalypse... It's an endless list. Is your bag befitting of such essential booty? Just look at it. Dull, bland, beige and plain. What were you thinking when you bought something practical and not pretty?

'Bovver' is London slang for a bit of trouble, and trouble is what you need. Shove your knitted colours in the face of fellow commuters with their drab luggage and boorish black briefcases. Your boring bag cries out for Bag Bovver; clout, character, and a giant helping of 'Oi! Cast yer mince pies over this blinder, me old mucker!' Knit one or I'll send the boys round for your kneecaps.

Difficulty rating: Tourist
Size: Depends on your bag
Gauge: You will need to work this out as part of calculating the right size bovver for your bag — see pattern instructions

WORKING OUT SIZE OF BAG BOVVER

The size of your bit of Bag Bovver depends on the bag you want to bovver up. Before you start knitting, you need to grab your tape measure, a pen, a notebook with something like 'Knitting Stuff' scrawled on the cover, and your brain.

> Knit a Bag Bovver that says 'Baby on Board' and shove some of your stash up your jumper in order to snag free seats on crowded tube trains.

1 Measure the area you want to add your Bag Bovver to. You don't have to be exact, but it's best to try to shoot for smaller than your space than bigger. Remember that knitting is a stretchy beast.

2 Write 'My Bag Bovver' at the top of a page, scribble down a name for your patch and WRITE DOWN YOUR MEASUREMENT. I mean it. If you don't, you'll have to do alllll this again when you want to make a new Bag Bovver patch. Your future self will want to punch you.

3 Decide what kind of pattern you're going to use on your Bag Bovver patch. Steal a stitch pattern from a favourite past knit, go for something plain, decide to attempt a fancy knit. It's up to you. Write down the pattern in your shiny notebook, along with the yarn you're using and the needle size.

4 Here comes the boring bit: knit yourself a gauge swatch 12 x 12cm (4¾ x 4¾in) in the same pattern you're going to use for the Bag Bovver patch.

5 Grab a calculator and tape measure. Work out how many stitches you need to knit 1cm (⅜in). Do it. Go on. It's boring but it'll mean your Bag Bovver fits perfectly. Write this down.

6 Now some easy maths. Multiply the number of stitches in 1cm (you just wrote that down, right?) by the width in cm of the area you want your Bag Bovver to cover. The total is the number of stitches you need to cast on to make your Bag Bovver the perfect size. Stitches per 1cm x width of Bag Bovver area = number of stitches you need to cast on.

7 Or you can just wing it. But don't come crying to me when you've knit 30 rows and it's too wide. If you do wing it, at least scribble down how many stitches you needed.

8 Knit knit knit knit knit knit knit.

9 Check halfway through to see if it looks as though it will fit.

10 Knit knit knit knit knit knit knit knit.

11 Loosely cast off (bind off) when your patch is long enough. Remember that casting off adds an extra bit of length, so cast off with a bit of room between your last row and the edge.

12 Write down how many rows you knit to make the patch.

13 Darn in ends. Yaaaaaaaaaaawn.

14 See if your Bag Bovver patch fits. Feel free to swear a bit if it doesn't, but it does serve you right for not checking halfway.

15 Knit, snip, sew and stick all kinds of everything onto your patch.

16 Sew two long strips of Velcro (hook side only) to the top and bottom of where you want your patch to be placed on your bag.

> Use Bag Bovver to chide starey fellow commuters who gawp at you when you knit by adding the words 'STOP STARING AT MY KNITS!'

If you think it needs some at the sides too, then go ahead. Usually top and bottom should do, though.

17 Press your Bag Bovver patch onto the Velcro strips. The yarn should stick to the Velcro no problem; there's no need to sew Velcro onto the Bag Bovver patch.

18 Swing your Bovvered Bag about your head like a tribal warrior. Whoop with triumph. Try not to scare the cat.

Voilà! Your first bit of Bag Bovver and a Bag Bovver blueprint for your bag. For each new patch, scribble down a new name, important stuff like yarn used and stitch pattern info, and any other useful bits. Your Bag Bovver blueprint will help a squillion new patches slide off your needles with the greatest of ease.

FLYING THE FLAG BAG BOVVER

The Flying the Flag Bag Bovver is really rather British. It's made for a rectangular or square bag and is knit in simple layers of colour sewn one of top of the other to produce a proud-to-be-British Union Jack. It smacks of Queen, Country, Cricket and Roast Beef. Huzzah!

> Beware of proclaiming your love for Star Trek/an X-Factor contestant/U2 with your Bag Bovver. Some loves are best kept to yourself. Okay?

Yarn

Your yarn quantities will differ for every bag. You'll need enough blue to knit your base rectangle or square, then about half that amount of white and a quarter that amount of red.
Red acrylic DK (worsted) yarn
White acrylic DK (worsted) yarn
Blue acrylic DK (worsted) yarn

PATTERN

Scottish Blue

Knit a garter stitch square or rectangle in blue yarn. (Write down how many sts you knit.)

Scottish White (make 4)

Cast on 6 sts in white yarn.
K in garter stitch until strip stretches from one corner to centre of patch. (Write down how many rows you knit.)
K2tog, k2, k2tog (4 sts).
K2tog twice (2 sts).
Thread yarn through sts.

Welsh Red (narrow red strips; make 4)

Cast on 4 sts in red yarn.
K in garter stitch until strip is same length as Scottish White.
Cast off (bind off).

English White (vertical strip)

Cast on 8 sts in white yarn.
K in garter stitch until strip stretches from top to bottom of patch.
Cast off (bind off).

English White (horizontal strip)

Cast on same number of sts as Scottish Blue in white yarn.
K 9 rows.
Cast off (bind off).

Americans: they make star-shaped buttons, y'know. Way easier than embroidery.

English Red (vertical strip)

Cast on 6 sts in red yarn.
K in garter stitch until strip stretches from top to bottom of patch.
Cast off (bind off).

English Red (horizontal strip)

Cast on same number of sts as Scottish Blue in red yarn.
K 6 rows.
Cast off (bind off).

FINISHING

Sew Scottish White strips to Scottish Blue patch with pointed ends sewn at corners.

Sew Welsh Red to Scottish White in the right places along edges: (clockwise from top left) bottom, top, top, bottom.
Sew English White strips across the centre.
Sew English Red strips across the centre on top of White.
Stand up and give a booming rendition of 'God Save the Queen'.

Use sew-on Velcro. Stick-on Velcro comes off. I have no idea why they call it 'stick-on'.

Clockwise from top left:
Purly Queen: Black DK (worsted) yarn, buttons, buttons and more buttons.
Luv a Duck Flypast: Sky-blue DK (worsted) yarn, I-cord cloud, feathered fellow, plastic aeroplane buttons and dotty handmade buttons for that shocked-duck look.
Twisty Thames: City-grey DK (worsted) yarn and Thames-flavoured river-coloured ribbon yarn.
Hyde Park Hive: Grass-green DK (worsted) yarn, bee buttons, flower buttons and lots of loop stitch.
Badly Drawn Bus: Red DK (worsted) yarn, white and yellow felt, big wheel buttons, and bold black very bad blanket stitch.

ALL CHANGE

When you get weary of your chosen Bovver, tear it off with wild abandon and reinvent your bag with a whole new bit of Bovver. Knit festive Bovver for Christmas, geeky Bovver to profess your love of Space Invaders, cryptic coded Bovver to pass on messages to spies, surreal Bovver to confuse onlookers, and marriage proposal Bovver to snag the one you love. One bag, infinite possibilities, and the chance to show off all kinds of stitching. Why didn't someone think of this before?

"Work Work Work

Hot tea, possible fur ball...

London is overrun with shiny-shoed, smart-suited office types. They're squeezed into cubicles, conference rooms and shared kitchens, from the City's Square Mile to the shiny skyscrapers of Canary Wharf. The London office is a place for occasional stationery stealing, paper plane desk wars, sneaky games of Facebook Scrabble, munching a multitude of returning-from-holiday biscuits, constant covert birthday card signing, and endless cups of hot and heavenly tea.

Your office is your home from home. Except that it's full of odd people and staple guns, and it isn't a good idea to spend all day in your pajamas there. Since you're going to spend a large chunk of your week at the office, you may as well get comfy with a bit of knitting. Keep your laptop cosy by slipping on a **Laptop Sock**, and warn off kitchen thieves and avoid cold tea with a **Mug Hugger** or two.

Yaaaaaarn, me hearties!

LAPTOP SOCK

Your little laptop is a window to online London: a place to find out where the best greasy spoon in Soho lurks; seek out the secret spots of sneaky Space Invader graffiti; hash over which yarn shop to spend half your wages in; tweet the fact that you sat opposite a reality TV washout on the Docklands Light Railway, and spy on those pesky Trafalgar Square pigeons via webcam.

If your socks treat your feet after a long London wander then surely your laptop should be treated too, for toting you through the virtual city. A Laptop Sock will express your unending love for your portable personal computer, and it's an excuse to get more knits out in the office. Win–win.

GUBBINS

Needles
4.5mm 40cm-long circular needle (US size 7, 16in long)
2.5mm (US B1/C2) crochet hook for button loops

Yarn
50g (1¾oz) DK (worsted) acrylic yarn in colour(s) of your choice
Small amount(s) of DK (worsted) yarn in colour(s) of your choice for embellishments

Other bits
Fabric glue or sewing thread for embellishments
3 buttons
Felt, eyes, Godzilla parts (optional)

Difficulty: Tourist
Size: Approx. 17 x 38cm (6¾ x 15in), but depends on your laptop (mine was made for a MacBook)
Gauge: 15 sts and 24 rows = 10cm (4in) in st st

PATTERN NOTES

The Laptop Sock stretches from 17cm (6¾in) wide flat to fit very snugly around a 23cm-wide (9in) laptop. If your laptop is much bigger, you'll need to add a few more stitches until the Sock stretches enough. You can test it out after a few inches to check.

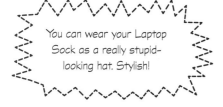

You can wear your Laptop Sock as a really stupid-looking hat. Stylish!

PATTERN

Cast on 52 sts in the yarn of your choice.
Place marker at start of row, join to knit in the round. (It might be a bit sticky to knit around to begin with, but it'll get easier once you're a few rows in.)
K till piece measures approx. 37cm (14½in), or more if your laptop is wider. You can carefully try your laptop sock on your laptop to check whether it's long enough.

The Laptop Sock may seem a little tight to pull on at first. It'll get easier with a few uses. Don't make the mistake of adding extra stitches, or you'll have a saggy baggy laptop sock and people will point and laugh.

Last 4 Rows
*K2, p2, rep from * around.
Cast off (bind off) loosely in pattern.

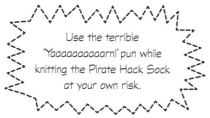

Use the terrible 'Yaaaaaaaaaarn!' pun while knitting the Pirate Hack Sock at your own risk.

Button Loops
Make three evenly spaced loops at one end of the Main Body.
For each loop chain 10 sts with 2.5mm (US B1/C2) crochet hook.
Sew loop back in 5mm (¼in) from start.

FINISHING

Sew up cast-on end.
Sew three buttons onto front of Sock 4cm (1½in) under rib to correspond to loops. Slip onto laptop and button up, tucking in the front before you button to cover top.
Marvel at how something so skinny can fit your lovely laptop.

Try saying 'Laptop Sock' really fast six times. The words lose all meaning.

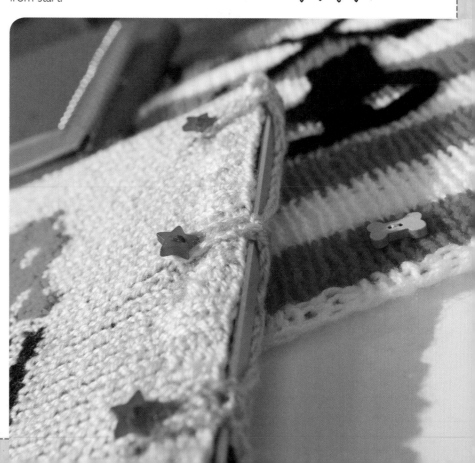

Pirate Hack Sock: Red and white DK (worsted) yarn in 8-row stripes with black DK (worsted) yarn I-cord for skull and crossbones.

Invader LDN Sock: Light blue, red and black DK (worsted). See The Tell-Tale Chart for the intarsia chart. Sample made smaller to fit an iPad.

Woolly Godzilla Sock: Green DK (worsted) yarn with white felt teeth, orange safety eyes, heroic aeroplane buttons, green felt spines and city-smashing claws.

The Invader LDN Sock is a knitted nod to French graffiti god Invader. There are more than 100 of his sneaky Space Invader mosaics around London.

The Woolly Godzilla sock needs to be kept well fed or he will turn on you one day and possibly eat your favourite handknit and one of your cats. Sorry about that.

ALL CHANGE

To add your own intarsia pattern, you can flatten out the laptop sock, add two stitches to each end for the seam, grab your grid paper and design your intarsia pattern from stitch 4–25 between row 15 and 65 - or the first and last 5cm (2in) - of the front of your Laptop Sock. Then sew up the side seam and bottom to make your sock.

Stitch for your smartphone by scaling down the Laptop Sock to smartphone size and losing one of the buttonholes. If your MP3 player, iPad or e-book reader gets jealous, you can make a sock for them too.

MUG HUGGERS

Tea. It's a liquid that runs caffeine-infused through the bloodstream of all England. Hot, brown and a miracle cure for all ills, the blood of most Londoners is 80% steaming hot tea. The drinking of tea in the office is an essential part of the office beast's biscuit-dunking, milk-stealing, sugar-adding, drink-slurping routine.

Your mug is your key to office relaxation: an excuse to stop pretending to work and indulge in a nice cuppa. At all costs, you must keep your mug from the sticky stealing mitts of those who can't be bothered to wash up their own. You could purchase a cup-sized chihuahua to sit in your mug and growl menacingly, or you could knit yourself a territorial Mug Hugger.

Designed to keep your drink piping hot and stamp your identity on your tea-toting chalice, the Mug Hugger comes in six cockney rhyming slang flavours: Dog and Bone (phone), Frog and Toad (road), Bees and Honey (money), Rabbit and Pork (talk), Apples and Pears (stairs), and Cat and Mouse (house).

Warn off a kitchen tea leaf (thief) who might half-inch (pinch) your mug for their own rosie lee (tea). Go on, gercha!

GUBBINS

Needles
Pair of 3.5mm (US size 4) needles
Pair of 3.5mm (US size 4) double-pointed needles
2.25mm (US B1) crochet hook
3.5mm (US E4) crochet hook

Yarn
25g (⅞oz) DK (worsted) acrylic yarn for main colour
Small amount of DK (worsted) acrylic yarn for additions

Other bits
Buttons for fastening
Safety eyes
See individual patterns for the rest

Difficulty rating: Tourist
Size: 17 x 10cm (6½ x 4in) but can stretch to fit 30cm (12in), and probably a bit bigger too
Gauge: 24.5 sts and 26 rows = 10cm (4in) in rib

PATTERN NOTES

The pattern for the Basic Mug Hugger Body and Button Loops is the basis for all six variations shown here. You can use this basic pattern as a starting point for your own creature creations.

BASIC PATTERN

Basic Mug Hugger Body

Cast on 42 sts using alternate cable cast-on (see The Way of the Knit).
Row 1 *K, p, rep from * across row.
Rows 2–26 Rep row 1.
Cast off (bind off) loosely in pattern.

Basic Mug Hugger Button Loops

Make three loops at one end of the Body.
You can use the threads from your cast-off (bound-off) and cast-on ends to make the top and bottom button loops.
For each loop, chain 12 sts using a 2.25mm (US B1) crochet hook.
Sew loop back in 5mm (¼in) from start.

Cast off loosely. Your Mug Hugger needs to stretch. It's a springy creature.

DOG AND BONE

Yarn

25g (⅞oz) brown variegated DK (worsted) yarn for body, legs and tail
Small amount of black DK (worsted) yarn for ears and nose
Small amount of red DK (worsted) yarn for tongue

Other bits

3 × wooden bone-shaped buttons
2 × safety eyes

Front Legs (make 2)

Cast on 3 sts in brown variegated yarn.
Push sts to other end of needle.
K 8 rows as I-cord (see The Way of the Knit).
Row 9 K, inc1, k (4 sts).
Rows 10–11 Knit as I-cord.
Thread yarn through sts.

Back Legs (make 2)

Cast on 3 sts in brown variegated yarn.
Push sts to other end of needle.
K 25 rows as I-cord
Rep rows 9–11 of Front Legs.
Thread yarn through sts.

Ears (make 2)

Using 3.5mm (US E4) crochet hook, chain 20 sts in black yarn.

Tongue

Cast on 5 sts in red yarn.
Work 6 rows in st st.

Row 7 K2tog, k, k2tog (3 sts).
Thread yarn through sts.

Nose

Cast on 6 sts in black yarn.
Rows 1–2 K across.
Row 3 K2tog, k2, k2tog (4 sts).
Row 4 K2tog, k2tog (2 sts).
Thread yarn through sts.

Tail

Chain 12 sts with 3.5mm (US E4) crochet hook in brown variegated yarn.

FINISHING

Sew on four legs, ears and nose.
Sew on tongue, tail and buttons.
Add eyes.
Scratch behind ears.

Make sure you add features and embroidery while the Mug Hugger is stretched out. If you do it before, it'll look horribly deformed when you do stretch it.

FROG AND TOAD

Yarn

25g (⅞oz) neon green DK (worsted) yarn for body and legs
Small amount of red DK (worsted) yarn for lips

Other bits

Stitch holder
3 × plastic toad buttons
2 × safety eyes

Front Legs (make 2)

Cast on 3 sts in neon green yarn.
Push sts to other end of needle.
K 8 rows as I-cord (see The Way of the Knit).

To make toes:
K first st, put 2 sts on holder.
K 2 rows on first st. Fasten off.
Take second stitch off holder.
K 3 rows on second st. Fasten off.
K 3 rows on third stitch. Fasten off.

Back Legs (make 2)

As Front Legs with 25 rows instead of 8.

Lips

Cast on 2 sts in red yarn.
Push sts to other end of needle.
K 50 rows as I-cord.
Thread yarn through sts and fasten off.

FINISHING

Sew on four legs, lips and buttons.
Add eyes.
Feed flies occasionally.

BEES AND HONEY

Yarn

25g (⅞oz) yellow and black DK (worsted) yarn for body, legs, arms and antennae
Small amount of white DK (worsted) yarn for wings

Other bits

2 × wooden beehive buttons
1 × bee button
2 × safety eyes

Body colour pattern

Start with yellow yarn and change colour at rows 7, 11, 17 and 21.

Wings (make 2)

Using 3.5mm (US E4) crochet hook chain 20 sts in white yarn.

Legs and Arms (make 6)

Using 3.5mm (US E4) crochet hook chain 7 sts in black yarn.
Sew yarn through end 12 times before knotting to make feet and hands.

Make sure you leave long tail to sew ends of hands and feet.

Antennae (make 2)

Using 2.25mm (US B1) crochet hook chain 6 sts in black.
Sew yarn through end 8 times before knotting to make tip.

FINISHING

Sew on legs, arms, wings and antennae.
Sew on buttons.
Add eyes.
Take somewhere flowery and let it buzz around.

RABBIT AND PORK

Yarn

25g (⅞oz) neon pink DK (worsted) yarn for body, legs and ears
Small amount of black DK (worsted) yarn for nose
Small amount of white DK (worsted) yarn for feet, teeth and pompom tail

APPLES AND PEARS

Yarn
25g (⅞oz) purple DK (worsted) yarn

Other bits
Red and green felt for fruit shapes
Yellow embroidery thread
2 x red plastic buttons
1 x green plastic button
4 x seed beads for eyes

FINISHING

Cut apple shape from red felt.
Cut pear shape from green felt.
Sew on using blanket stitch and yellow
embroidery thread.
Sew on eyes and buttons.
Challenge to staring competition.

Other bits
3 x wooden pig-shaped buttons
2 x safety eyes

Front Legs (make 2)
Cast on 3 sts in neon pink yarn.
Push sts to other end of needle.
K 8 rows as I-cord (see The Way
of the Knit).
Change yarn to white.
Row 8 K as I-cord.
Row 9 K, inc1, k (4 sts).
Rows 10–11 K as I-cord.
Thread yarn through sts.

Back Legs (make 2)
Cast on 3 sts in neon pink yarn.
Push sts to other end of needle.
K 23 rows as I-cord
Change to white yarn.
Rep rows 8–11 of Front Legs.
Thread yarn through sts.

Ears (make 2)
Cast on 7 sts in neon pink yarn.

Rows 1–25 Work in st st.
Thread yarn through all sts.

Teeth
Cast on 4 sts in white yarn.
Work 4 rows in st st.
Cast off (bind off).

Nose
Cast on 6 sts in black yarn.
Rows 1–2 K across.
Row 3 K2tog, k2, k2tog (4 sts).
Row 4 K2tog, k2tog (2 sts).
Thread yarn through sts.

Tail
Make small white pompom (see
The Way of the Knit).

FINISHING

Sew on four legs, nose, ears and tail.
Sew on teeth with knit side at front.
Embroider vertical line in black yarn.
Add eyes.
Offer carrot.

CAT AND MOUSE

Yarn

25g (⅞oz) white DK (worsted) yarn and 25g (⅞oz) white faux fur yarn
Small amount of pink DK (worsted) yarn for nose
Small amount of blue yarn for collar

Other bits

2 × plastic mouse buttons
1 × 'meow' button
1 × silver bell
2 × cat safety eyes

Front Legs (make 2)

Cast on 3 sts holding together white yarn and faux fur yarn.
Push sts to other end of needle.
K 8 rows as I-cord (see The Way of the Knit).
Row 9 K, inc1, k (4 sts).
Rows 10–11 K as I-cord.
Thread yarn through sts.

Back Legs (make 2)

Cast on 3 sts holding together white yarn and faux fur yarn.
Push sts to other end of needle.
K 25 rows as I-cord.
Rep rows 9–11 of Front Legs.
Thread yarn through sts.

Ears (make 2)

Cast on 7 sts holding together white yarn and faux fur yarn.
Rows 1–8 Work in st st.

Row 9 K2tog, k3, k2tog (5 sts).
Row 10 P2tog, p, p2tog (3 sts).
Thread yarn through all sts.

Nose

Cast on 6 sts in pink yarn.
Rows 1–2 K across.
Row 3 K2tog, k2, k2tog (4 sts).
Row 4 K2tog, k2tog (2 sts).
Thread yarn through sts.

Tail

Cast on 2 sts holding together white yarn and faux fur yarn.
Push sts to other end of needle.
K 10 rows as I-cord.
Thread yarn through sts.

Collar

Chain 55 sts with 3.5mm (US E4) crochet hook in blue yarn.

FINISHING

Sew on four legs, nose, ears and tail.
Sew on buttons.
Add eyes and collar.
Give saucer of milk till purring ensues.

ALL CHANGE

Mug Huggers can be simple, stylish and chic with no embellishments and a few fancy buttons. But what fun would that be? Mess with the ears, eyes, skinny little I-cord legs and yarns to create a mug-hugging beast of your own.

You can mug-hug pretty much anything: vases, pencil pots, beer bottles, lampposts, jam jars, those street performers who stand still for hours, or pirates' wooden legs. Add stitches to the length or width of the pattern to mug-hug all kinds of things. Gift-wrap a wine bottle as a gorilla, pretty up a plant pot as a giant panda, cosy your coffee pot, or add a great white shark hugger to London's Gherkin building (that last one may take a while, and you're going to need bigger needles).

City Critters

Londoners aren't just two-legged. They're two-winged, four-pawed, two-footed (if they avoid foot-mangling calamity) and sharp-beaked. They have twitchy ears, manky toes, scritchy claws and whisky tails. They're our shadow slinkers, our bin raiders, our bread-crust-pecking beggars and our alarm-call caw-ers at 6 in the morning when you thought you were the only one up. Criss-crossing the city, wild Londoners are as much a part of life as the rat-race human beings.

Introducing four of London's feral fibre folk to help turn wild London woolly: plucky **Cooey the Pigeon**, treasonous **Grog the Raven**, twitchy **Toerag the Tube Mouse** and fleet-footed **Fleabag the Fox**.

Cooey longed for an abandoned sandwich crust.

COOEY THE PIGEON

London's pigeons are legend. From the days when a practically perfect Nanny taking care of two brats in long-gone Edwardian London sang 'Feeeeeeeed the biiiiiiiiirds, Tuppence a baaaaaaaaaaag!'; to the tragic tale of the evil pigeon-eating pelican of St James Park; to the few that flap clumsily in the face of danger in Trafalgar Square despite the iron claws of the anti-pigeon falcons; to the bobbing-headed brave I once saw hop on a train at Mansion House tube station just before the doors shut. I have no idea if he had a ticket. I suspect he didn't.

Cooey the Pigeon is a tribute to manky London pigeons everywhere. Long may they hobble about on their mangled pink feet; decorate the heads of our dignitaries with their whitewash; and live on to peck at our discarded 3 a.m. kebab remains.

Difficulty rating: London Local
Size: Approx. 9cm (3½in) tall
Gauge: Not important

GUBBINS

Needles
Set of four 3.5mm (US size 4) double-pointed needles or circular needle for magic loop (see The Way of the Knit)

Yarn
15g (½oz) blue-grey DK (worsted) yarn for body and wings
Small amount of white DK (worsted) yarn for wing stripes
Small amount of yellow (worsted) yarn DK for embroidering beak

Other bits
Stitch marker
Stuffing
2 x 15cm-long (6in) pink pipe cleaners for feet
Black beads for eyes
Glue

PATTERN

Body

Cast on 3 sts in blue-grey yarn.
Push sts to other end of needle.
Row 1 Inc1 three times as I-cord
(see The Way of the Knit) (6 sts).
Divide sts between three needles, place
marker at start of round and join to
knit in the round.
Round 2 K around.
Round 3 K1, inc1 each needle (9 sts).
Round 4 K around.
Round 5 K2, inc1 each needle (12 sts).
Round 6 K around.
Round 7 K3, inc1 each needle (15 sts).
Rounds 8–12 K around.
Round 13 K4, inc1 each needle (18 sts).
Round 14 K around.
Round 15 K around.
Round 16 (K2, inc1) twice each needle
(24 sts).
Round 17 K around.
Round 18 K around.

Make hundreds of pigeons, perch them all over a school climbing frame, then run around screaming to reenact a scene from Hitchcock's 'The Birds'.

Roll stuffing and stuff head.

Round 19 K around.
Round 20 (K3, inc1) twice each needle
(30 sts).
Round 21 K around.
Round 22 K around.
Round 23 (K3, k2tog) twice each needle
(24 sts).

Round 24 K.
Round 25 (K2, k2tog) twice each
needle (18 sts).

Roll stuffing and stuff body.

Wear your pigeon on your shoulder to give yourself that urban pirate look.

Round 26 K around.
Round 27 K2tog around (9 sts).
Thread yarn through all sts.

You could roll your pigeon in an ashtray to give it that authentic filthy London smell. You'd be a bit of a nutter, though.

Wings (make 2)

Cast on 5 sts in blue-grey yarn.
Row 1 K across.
Row 2 P across.
Row 3 Sl1, k4.
Row 4 P across.
Row 5 Sl1, k4.
Row 6 P across.
Change colour to white yarn.
Row 7 K across.
Row 8 P across.
Change colour to blue-grey yarn.
Row 9 K across.
Row 10 P2tog, p, p2tog (3 sts).
Row 11 K across.
Thread yarn through sts.

If you cut a pipe cleaner with scissors, make sure you bend the cut end to make it rounded. Cut pipe cleaner ends are scratchy.

FINISHING

Sew on wings.
Embroider beak with yellow yarn.
Add eyes.
Bend pipe cleaners to form feet
(see www.knitthepigeon.com
for instructions).
Dab glue onto leg ends of pipe
cleaners and push into body.
Offer stale kebab leftovers.

The city has a hundred ways to mangle the ever-present pigeon. Chop off a toe to add authenticity.

ALL CHANGE

Knit Cooey in pink and she's a rare Mauritian pink pigeon of paradise. Knit her in white, stick an olive branch in her beak and she's a dove. Add a little punk styling and you've got Australia's crested pigeon on your needles. Stick on two extra eyes and another beak and she's the horrific freak pigeon you hoped you'd never see. Oh the horror.

GROG THE RAVEN

Strong foundations are all well and good, but if you don't have a handful of ravens then your nation is a wobbly thing. The city's Tower of London is home to seven feathered fellows who hold the fate of the city in their pointy beaks. It is whispered about the Tower's hallowed historic halls that 'If the Tower of London ravens are lost or fly away, the Crown will fall and Britain with it.'

This little knit celebrates Grog the Raven. A bird who, after 21 years of service to the crown, left his post and nipped off down the pub, thus bringing shame upon the feathered fellows of the Tower in 1981. Just goes to show that you can clip a true Londoner's wings and tempt them to stay with regular meals of blood-soaked biscuits, but when a Londoner wants a pint, they want a pint. Hic.

GUBBINS
Needles

Set of four 3.5mm (US size 4) double-pointed needles or circular needle for magic loop (see The Way of the Knit)

Yarn
15g (½oz) black DK (worsted) yarn

Other bits
Stitch marker
Stuffing
Black safety eyes, one big and one small
2 x 15cm-long (6in) black pipe cleaners
Glue

Difficulty rating: London Local
Size: Approx. 9cm (3½in) tall
Gauge: Not important

PATTERN

Body

Cast on 3 sts in black yarn.
Push sts to other end of needle.
Row 1 Incl three times as I-cord (see The Way of the Knit) (6 sts).
Divide sts between three needles, place marker at start of round and join to knit in the round.
Round 2 K around.
Round 3 K1, incl each needle (9 sts).
Round 4 K around.

Get Grog to buy the first round if you do go drinking with him. He's been known to conveniently forget whose round it is after a few.

Round 5 K2, incl each needle (12 sts).
Round 6 K around.
Round 7 K3, incl each needle (15 sts).
Round 8 K around.

Round 9 K4, incl each needle (18 sts).
Rounds 10–14 K around.
Round 15 (K2, incl) twice each needle (24 sts).
Round 16 K around.
Round 17 K around.
Round 18 (K3, incl) twice each needle (30 sts).
Round 19 K around.
Round 20 K around.

Roll stuffing into ball and stuff head.

Round 21 K around.
Round 22 (K4, inc1) twice each needle (36 sts).
Rounds 23–28 K around.
Round 29 (K4, k2tog) twice each needle (30 sts).
Round 30 K around.
Round 31 (K3, k2tog) twice each needle (24 sts).
Round 32 K around.
Round 33 K2tog around (12 sts).

Roll stuffing and stuff body.

Round 34 K.
Round 35 K2tog around (6 sts).

Thread yarn through all sts.

<u>Wings (make 2)</u>
Cast on 5 sts in black yarn.
Row 1 K across.
Row 2 P across.
Row 3 Sl1, k4.
Row 4 Sl1, p4.
Row 5 Sl1, k4.
Row 6 Sl1, p4.
Row 7 Sl1, inc1, k, inc1, k (7 sts).
Row 8 Sl1, p6.
Row 9 Sl1, k6.
Row 10 P2tog, p3, p2tog (5 sts).
Row 11 Sl1, k4.
Row 12 P2tog, p, p2tog (3 sts).

Thread yarn through sts.

<u>Beak</u>
Cast on 8 sts in black yarn.
Row 1 K across.
Row 2 P across.
Row 3 K across.
Row 4 P across.
Row 5 K across.
Row 6 P across.
Row 7 Sl1, k3, k2tog, k (7 sts). Turn.
Row 8 Sl1, p, p2tog, p (6 sts). Turn.
Row 9 Sl1, k2tog, k across (5 sts).
Row 10 P3, p2tog (4 sts).
Row 11 K2tog twice (2 sts).
Row 12 P2tog (1 st).
Thread yarn through st.

You can use two eyes the same size, but that won't give Grog that boozy look, and who wants a respectable-looking raven?

ALL CHANGE
In green with hints of tropical orange, Grog has been known to sail the seven seas with many a scurvy crew. Be sure to pack at least eight pieces of eight and some limes for the scurvy before you send him seawards.

<u>FINISHING</u>

Sew on wings and beak.
Add eyes.
Bend pipe cleaners to form feet.
Dab glue onto leg ends of pipe cleaner and push into body.
Offer to take to pub.

Sew the wingtips to Grog's body for that haughty air.

TOERAG THE TUBE MOUSE

There is no outrage quite like the outrage a Londoner feels when we have to wait more than two minutes for a tube train. Don't they know who we are?! We have places to go. People to see. We don't have time to stand about down here in the belly of London waiting for trains. Grrr!

There is only one cure for this subterranean rage, and it comes on four pattering paws with a twitching nose delicately attuned to the wafting scent of still-warm, greasy, vinegar-soaked chip-shop leavings. A sighting of the humble London tube mouse whisks you from the shadows of rumbling under-London to the hushed happiness of finding yourself unexpectedly in a wildlife documentary.

Toerag the tube mouse: sooty furred with underground filth, hard of hearing due to endless ear-shattering train thunder, and reluctant to pause for pictures, but proof that even in London's dusty undercarriage there's still something to smile about.

GUBBINS

Needles
Set of four 3.5mm (US size 4) double-pointed needles or circular needle for magic loop (see The Way of the Knit)

Yarn
15g (½oz) grey DK (worsted) yarn for body
Small amount of light pink DK (worsted) yarn for ears, back feet, tail and front paws
Small amount of black DK (worsted) yarn for nose

Other bits
Stitch marker
Stuffing
Black beads for eyes

Difficulty rating: London Local
Size: Approx. 9cm (3½in) tall
Gauge: Not important

PATTERN

Body

Cast on 3 sts in grey yarn.
Push sts to other end of needle.
Row 1 Inc1 three times as I-cord
(see The Way of the Knit) (6 sts).
Divide sts between three needles, place
marker at start of round and join to
knit in the round.
Round 2 Inc1 around (12 sts).
Round 3 K around.
Round 4 Inc1 around (24 sts).
Round 5 K around.
Round 6 (K3, inc1) twice each needle
(30 sts).

Rounds 7–12 K around.
Round 13 (K3, k2tog) twice each
needle (24 sts).
Round 14 K around.
Round 15 K around.
Round 16 (K2, k2tog) twice each
needle (18 sts).
Round 17 K around.
Round 18 K around.

Roll stuffing and stuff body.

Rounds 19–23 K around.
Round 24 K15.
Skp.
Turn.

Sl1, p3, p2tog.
Turn.
K to end of row (16 sts).
Round 25 K around.

Roll stuffing and stuff neck.

Round 26 K2tog, k5, k2tog, k around
(14 sts).
Round 27 K2tog, k3, k2tog, k around
(12 sts).
Round 28 K2tog, k, (k2tog) twice, k3,
k2tog (8 sts).

Stuff head.

Round 29 K around.
Round 30 K3, k2tog, k, k2tog (6 sts).
Round 31 (K2tog) three times (3 sts).

Thread yarn through sts.

Make a fellow tube-mouse
admirer's day: add to the tube
mouse population by knitting
a tube mouse and wildly
abandoning him somewhere
on the Underground.

Tail

Cast on 3 sts in pink yarn.
Push sts to other end of needle.
K 15 rows I-cord.
Thread yarn through sts.

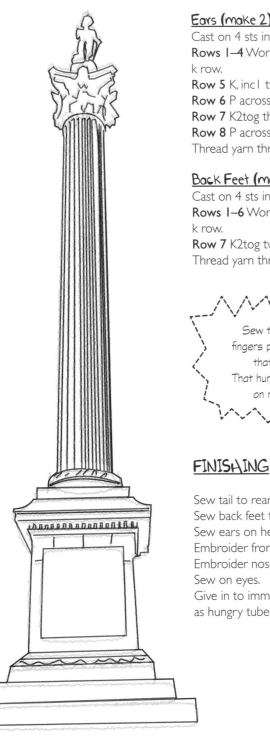

Ears (make 2)

Cast on 4 sts in light pink yarn.
Rows 1–4 Work in st st starting with k row.
Row 5 K, inc1 twice, k (6 sts).
Row 6 P across.
Row 7 K2tog three times (3 sts).
Row 8 P across.
Thread yarn through sts.

Back Feet (make 2)

Cast on 4 sts in light pink yarn.
Rows 1–6 Work in st st starting with k row.
Row 7 K2tog twice (2 sts).
Thread yarn through sts.

> Sew the paws with the fingers pointing upwards for that horrified 'Agh! That human is going to step on me!' expression.

FINISHING

Sew tail to rear of body.
Sew back feet to bottom of body.
Sew ears on head.
Embroider front paws.
Embroider nose with black yarn.
Sew on eyes.
Give in to immediate demand for food as hungry tube mouse comes to life.

ALL CHANGE

Use darker yarn with an extra stitch or two for the width of the tail and add a few rows to the nose to turn your tube mouse ratty. Be warned: Black Plague fleas made from beads may be historically correct, but will probably make people think you're a bit sick.

Knit your mouse in white and add a pair of intellectual glasses for lab-mouse chic.

> Make a really, really long tail and wrap it around the mouse like a scarf. If a real mouse had a tail that long, he'd do that too.

FLEABAG THE FOX

Pootle through the streets of late-night London when there's no one else around and you'll sometimes glimpse a pair of eyes reflected in the shadows. No, it's not Satan himself come to claim your soul after that foolish bargain you made with him over the rollerskates you wanted for your eighth birthday; it's most likely one of London's long-faced urban foxes.

Seeing a fox in the cool quiet of the after-hours city is a magical thing. Seeing him ripping through the bin bag outside your house for chicken scraps is less magical, and probably means you'll have to go out there in your slippers to tidy up before the neighbours complain.

Fleabag the Fox is a purled pointy-eared vulpine hero of the urban wild. Knit him proudly so he can bark at the moon, drink from your murky pond, and scare the pants off your cats (if your cats wore pants, which would look very odd) by appearing at the end of your garden and staring eerily towards the house…

GUBBINS

Needles
Set of four 3.5mm (US size 4) double-pointed needles or circular needle for magic loop (see The Way of the Knit)

Yarn
15g (½oz) orange DK (worsted) yarn for body, tail, front legs and back feet
Small amount of white DK (worsted) yarn for tail end and muzzle
Small amount of black DK (worsted) yarn for nose

Other bits
Stitch marker
Stuffing
Black beads for eyes

Difficulty rating: London Local
Size: Approx. 9cm (3½in) tall
Gauge: Not important

PATTERN

Body
Cast on 3 sts in orange yarn.
Push sts to other end of needle.
Row 1 Inc1 three times as I-cord
(see The Way of the Knit) (6 sts).
Divide sts between three needles, place
marker at start of round and join to
knit in the round.
Round 2 Inc1 around (12 sts).
Round 3 K around.
Round 4 Inc1 around (24 sts).
Round 5 K around.
Round 6 (K3, inc1) twice each needle
(30 sts).
Rounds 7–12 K around.
Round 13 (K3, k2tog) twice each
needle (24 sts).
Round 14 K around.
Round 15 K around.
Round 16 (K2, k2tog) twice each
needle (18 sts).
Round 17 K around.
Round 18 K around.

Roll stuffing and stuff body.

Round 19 K around.
Round 20 K3, change to white yarn,
k3, change to orange yarn, k around.
Rounds 21–22 Rep round 20.
Round 23 K2, change to white yarn,
k5, change to orange yarn, k around.
Row 24 K2, change to white yarn,
k5, change to orange yarn, k6.
Skp.
Turn.
Sl1, p3, p2tog.
Turn.
K to end of row (16 sts).
Round 25 K2, change to white yarn,
k5, change to orange yarn, k9.

Roll stuffing and stuff neck and head.

Round 26 K2tog, change to white yarn,
k5, change to orange yarn, k2tog, k7
(14 sts).
Round 27 Change to white yarn, k2tog,
k3, k2tog, change to orange yarn, k7
(12 sts).
Round 28 Change to white yarn, k2tog,
k, k2tog, change to orange yarn, k2tog,
k3, k2tog (8 sts).

Roll stuffing and stuff nose.

Round 29 Change to white yarn,
k around.
Round 30 K3, k2tog, k, k2tog (6 sts).
Round 31 K2tog three times (3 sts).

Thread yarn through sts.

Tail
Cast on 3 sts in orange yarn.
Push sts to other end of needle.
Row 1 K across as I-cord.
Row 2 Inc1 around (6 sts).
Divide sts between three needles, place
marker at start of round and join to
knit in the round.
Round 3 K around.
Round 4 Inc1 around (12 sts).
Rounds 5–10 K around.
Round 11 (K2tog, k) around (8 sts).

Change to white yarn.

Round 12 K around.

Stuff tail.

Round 13 K around.
Round 14 K2tog around (4 sts).
Round 15 K around.

Round 16 K2tog twice (2 sts).
Thread yarn through sts.

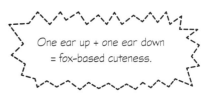

One ear up + one ear down
= fox-based cuteness.

Ears (make 2)
Cast on 4 sts in orange yarn.
Rows 1–7 Work in st st starting
with k row.
Row 8 P2tog twice (2 sts).
Row 9 K2.
Row 10 P2.
Thread yarn through sts.

Front legs (make 2)
Cast on 3 sts in orange yarn.
Push sts to other end of needle.
Rows 1–10 K as I-cord.
Row 11 Inc1 each st as I-cord (6 sts).
Row 12 K as I-cord.
Row 13 K as I-cord.
Row 14 K2tog three times as I-cord
(3 sts).
Thread yarn through sts.

Back Feet (make 2)
Cast on 4 sts in orange yarn.
Rows 1–6 Work in st st starting with
k row.
Row 7 K2tog twice (2 sts).
Thread yarn through sts.

Watch Fleabag around your bin
bags. He likes to rip into them,
and he is very reluctant to help
tidy up after.

FINISHING

Sew tail to rear of fox body.
Sew legs to front halfway up body.
Sew back feet to bottom of body.
Sew ears on head.
Embroider nose with black yarn.
Sew on eyes.
Compliment him on his fine bushy tail.
Foxes are very proud of them.

ALL CHANGE

Fleabag in sand-coloured yarn could be an Aussie dingo. Stitch him in grey and he's wolfish. Knit Fleabag in eyelash yarn and he's a street-hungry mongrel. Just don't forget to feed him. Hungry knitted hounds may chew your shoes.

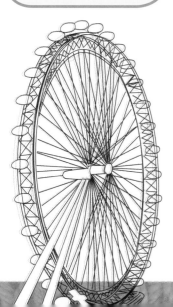

"The Great Outdoors"

London's weather gods laugh at your open-toed sandals, giggle at your fleece-lined bobble hat and guffaw at your trendy legwarmer-and-welly combo. They are a fickle, fiendish and often grumpy folk. Expecting sprinkling showers in spring, jacket-shunning sunshine in summer, chaos-causing leaves on train lines in autumn, and dank drizzle and snow flurries in winter? Maybe. But maybe not.

A savvy city dweller, on watching the grinning TV weatherperson wave their hands at cloudless skies, will shove on some shades, pack a picnic and then reach for their trusty brolly.

The best way to beat the London weather gods is to arm yourself for elemental war, knitwise. Prepare for a precipitation on your picnic with the **Parklife Plarn Picnic Blanket** (with the added bonus of going green while you garter stitch); festoon your foliage with waterproof **Plastic Bag Bugs**; and dance in the downpour with a ring of dangling **Umbrella Fellas**.

PARKLIFE PLARN PICNIC BLANKET

GUBBINS

Needles
Pair of 10mm (US size 17) needles

Yarn
To make the plarn (plastic bag yarn), you'll need plastic bags in many colours (don't use biodegradable ones). Thin plastic bags work much better than thick ones as they're softer, fold down smaller and are easier to knit.

Other bits
Good scissors
Fishing line or strong invisible thread (optional)
Patience
Picnic to eat on blanket
Security guard to prevent picnic ants or hungry cartoon bear invasion (optional)

From teeny-tiny Postman's Park to hulking Hyde Park, London's green spaces are tree-trimmed, duck-paddled, daisy-chained, squirrel-infested, grassy, pollen-puffing pieces of paradise. The merest hint of sunshine sees city dwellers rushing to our parks, discarding garments as they go, to bask pasty and goose-pimpled in Mother Nature's good works. We swat at wasps, toast ourselves sunburnt, make vague attempts at team sports and, most importantly, shove facefuls of chilled food and drink into our gobs.

A green knit for London's green spaces makes perfect sense. The Parklife Plarn Picnic Blanket offers you somewhere to sit and snarfle sausage rolls and strawberries. It laughs in the face of lesser picnic places. It's practically free, it squashes up small; it's stainproof, rainproof and surprisingly soft to sit on. It's also green, even when it's multicoloured. Save the planet and have a Scotch egg.
Picnic perfection for peanuts.

Difficulty rating: Tourist
Size: Up to you
Gauge: Not important

PATTERN NOTES

You'll first need to make the plarn.
1 Flatten out your plastic bag into a neat rectangle.
2 Fold your plastic bag in half lengthways and in half again.
3 Cut the handles and bottom off your plastic bag.

Making plarn can get horribly boring. Put something good on the TV before plarn-making commences. It's going to be a long night.

4 Chop your bag into strips 2cm (¾ in) wide.
5 Pull out the strips and lay two loops end one over the other. We'll call them A and B.
6 Pull right end of loop A up through loop B and feed the left end of loop A through the right end.
7 Pull both loops to tighten the knot, securing them together.
8 Repeat this over and over and then wind your ball of plarn.

Biodegradable plastic bags will turn to dust after being out in the sun for a while. To avoid horror, check your bag isn't biodegradable before you plarn it.

PATTERN

Cast on 10 sts.
K 15 rows.
Cast off (bind off).
Sew in ends.
Repeat for each square until you have as many squares as you want, or you run out of plarn, or you have knit so much plarn you start thinking it might make a nifty outfit if the plastic bags were nice enough.

Plarn is stretchy, so any tight stitches can be pulled loose.

If your plarn breaks it's usually okay to tie it back together, unless you're fussy about these things.

FINISHING

Sew all your plarn squares together with even more plarn, or use fishing line or strong invisible thread.
You can reinforce the blanket's edges with blanket stitch sewn in – you've guessed it – more plarn.
Test out your blanket by sitting on it and eating a packet of crisps and an apple. It doesn't matter which flavour the crisps are.

Keep your plastic bag ends and handles for stuffing or for Bag Bug wings (see pattern pages later). We're recycling here, so watch your waste or the Recycling Troll will curse you.

ALL CHANGE

Waterproof squares of plarn are useful things. In your bathroom they're bathmats; by the front door they're doormats; in the garden they're plant-pot stands with water-draining skills; on your balding uncle's head they're a really bad wig. Sew together as many or as few as you like and make plarn plans. Plarn squares make excellent pan scrubbers. You have to actually be there scrubbing to make it work, though. They won't scrub on their own if you leave them and go off to make tea.

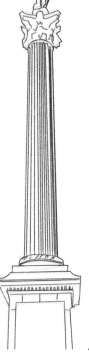

PLASTIC BAG BUGS

GUBBINS

Needles
Pair of 4.5mm (US size 7) needles

Yarn
1 bag made into 1cm-wide (⅜in) plarn (plastic bag yarn; see previous project for plarn-making instructions)

Other bits
Plastic bag bits for wings
Googly eyes
Glue (optional if eyes aren't sticky)
Invisible thread or fishing line
Tree to hang bugs from

London's bugs can grate on the nerves a bit. They chomp on your struggling seedlings, try to land on your lunch if you choose to eat al fresco and continually fly into the kitchen window glass on the right when the window on the left is wide open.

Luckily, these wind-dancing Plastic Bag Bugs are good for your patch of urban garden. They spin gracefully in the wind, put that pile of plastic bags to good use, and may even scare away seed-stealing birds. A swarm of them hanging from the trees in a stiff London breeze is a sight to behold.

Difficulty rating: Tourist
Size: About 10cm (4in) at longest or widest point
Gauge: Not important

PATTERNS

DOOBRIE THE DRAGONFLY

Body
Cast on 6 sts.
K 15 rows.
Row 16 K2tog three times. (3 sts).
K 3 rows.
Pull yarn through sts.
Sew up body, leaving mouth open.

Wings
Flatten and fold a plastic bag in half.
Cut wing shapes from folded plastic bag to make two identical long wings joined in the centre.
Use a crochet hook or a needle to pass wings through two of the back stitches on the body.
Smooth out wings.

Put spare googly eyes on random family photos around the house. It never stops being funny.

Slap a bit of glow-in-the-dark paint on your bugs to give them that 'aliens have landed' look.

BARMY THE BUTTERFLY

Body

Cast on 8 sts.
K 12 rows.
Row 13 K2tog four times. (4 sts).
K 2 rows.
Pull yarn through sts.
Sew up body, leaving mouth open.

Wings

Flatten and fold a plastic bag in half.
Cut wing shapes from folded plastic
bag to make two identical round wings
joined in the centre.
Use crochet hook or needle to pass
wings through two of the back stitches
on the body.
Smooth out wings.

> Tie your Bugs on securely.
> They're tame creatures and
> won't survive long on their
> own in the wilderness.

FINISHING

Add googly eyes.
Sew in antennae for butterfly and tail
for dragonfly using stretched-out plastic
to make it thin.
Sew invisible thread onto top of bug.
Dangle bug from something outdoors
and oooo and aaaaah at it spinning in
the wind.

> Different-sized googly eyes on
> the same bug will give them an
> unhinged cartoon-crazy stare.

ALL CHANGE

Bugs can become birds with a few feather-like additions
and a bit of a beak.

Add black and yellow stripes and a shortened body for a Bag
Bug Bee; go red, black and rounder for a Ladybird; and lengthen
and curl your purl for a Snail.

UMBRELLA FELLAS

Soggy London is sprinkled by rain about 15 days a month. We're like ducks: a people who are slightly damp, with frizzy hair and worryingly webbed feet (I lied about the feet). But us Londoners love the rain. You can keep your eternal sunshine and blue skies, because we have our drizzle, our puddles and an excuse to stroll about with one of the world's most ingenious inventions: the umbrella.

The umbrella is an indispensable London sidekick: wave it angrily at buses that pull away just as you puff and pant your way to the bus stop; lean on it casually when you fail to get a seat on your morning train; use it to shoo away gammy pigeons or ward off over-zealous free-newspaper shovers; and hide under it from the rain wrath of London's displeased weather gods.

Sling a handful of Umbrella Fellas at your rainproof pal and it becomes a cool and kooky canopy. Beautify your brolly with dangling Drips, flying Flurries, spinning Sprigs, lovey-dovey Flutters and spectral Spooks. Stand out from the sea of plain parasols and dance in the deluge with tiny flocks of fibre folk.

GUBBINS

Needles

Set of 2.5mm (US size 1) double-pointed needles or circular needle for magic loop (see The Way of the Knit)

Yarn
25g (⅞oz) acrylic 4ply (sport) yarn:
Pale blue for Drips
Mint green for Sprigs
White for Flurries and Spooks
Scarlet for Flutters
Any colour for Tidy

Other bits
Stuffing
Beads for eyes
Black embroidery thread for Spooks' mouths
Stitch holder for Flutters
An umbrella
Waterproofing spray (check out camping shops)
Strong invisible thread or fishing line
About 5cm (2in) of Velcro for Tidy

Difficulty: London Local
Size: 3cm (1¼in) long
Gauge: Not important

PATTERN NOTES

There are eight tips to most umbrellas, so knit eight Umbrella Fellas. You can knit them all the same or mix them up. Just make sure they're introduced to each other before tying them on. It's only polite.

PATTERNS

Drips (Raindrops)

Cast on 4 sts using pale blue yarn.
Push sts to other end of needle.
Row 1 Inc1 across as I-cord (see The Way of the Knit) (8 sts).
Divide sts on needles and join to knit in the round.
Round 2 K around.
Round 3 *K1, inc1, rep from * around (12 sts).
Round 4 K around.
Round 5 *K1, inc1, rep from * around (18 sts).
Rounds 6–7 K around.

Round 8 K2tog around (9 sts).
Round 9 K around.
Stuff.
Rounds 10–11 K around.
Round 12 K2tog, k, k2tog, k, k2tog, k (6 sts).
Round 13 K around.
Round 14 K2tog around (3 sts).
Thread yarn through sts.
Darn in ends.

Flurries (Snowflakes)

Step 1 Cast on 4 sts using white yarn.
Step 2 Lift 3 sts one by one over last st.
Step 3 Cast on 1 st.
Rep steps 1–3 until there are 16 cast-on sts.

K 2 rows.
Thread yarn through sts and pull tight.
Sew together two ends to form a circle.
Darn in ends.

Sprigs (Leaves)

Cast on 2 sts using mint green yarn.
Push sts to other end of needle.
K 3 rows as I-cord.
Row 4 K, m1, k (3 sts).
Row 5 P, k, p.
Row 6 Inc1, p, inc1 (5 sts).
Row 7 P2, k, p2.
Row 8 K, inc1, p, inc1, k (7 sts).
Row 9 P3, k, p3.
Row 10 K2, inc1, p, inc1, k2 (9 sts).
Row 11 P4, k, p4.

Flutters (Hearts)

Cast on 4 sts using scarlet yarn.
Divide sts on needles and join to knit in the round.
Round 1 Inc1 around (8 sts).
Round 2 K around.
Round 3 *K, inc1, inc1, k, rep from * (12 sts).
Round 4 K around.
Round 5 *K, inc1, k2, inc1, k, rep from * (16 sts).
Round 6 K around.
Round 7 *K, inc1, k4, inc1, k, rep from * (20 sts).
Round 8 K5, slip 10 sts onto a stitch holder, k5 (dividing the top of the Flutter into two).
Round 9 *K, k2tog, ssk, repeat from * (6 sts).
Round 10 K around.
Thread yarn through sts.
Lightly stuff Flutter.
Rejoin yarn to sts on stitch holder.

Rep rounds 9 and 10 for other side of Flutter.
Lightly stuff the rest of the Flutter.
Sew gap between two halves closed.

Spooks (Skulls)

Cast on 4 sts using white yarn.
Divide sts on needles and join to knit in the round.
Round 1 Inc1 around (8 sts).
Rounds 2–7 K around.
Round 8 *K, inc1, rep from * around (12 sts).
Round 9 K around.
Round 10 *K, inc1, rep from * around (18 sts).
Rounds 11–12 K around.
Round 13 *K2, inc1, rep from * around (24 sts).
Round 14 *K2, k2tog, rep from * around (18 sts).
Round 15 *K, k2tog, rep from * around (12 sts).

Keep the Fellas away from the cat. A chewed-up Umbrella Fella covered in cat spit is a traumatising sight.

Row 12 K4, p, K4.
Rows 13–17 Rep row 11 (odd rows) and row 12 (even rows).
Row 18 K2, k2tog, p, k2tog, k2 (7 sts).
Row 19 P, p2tog, k, p2tog, p (5 sts).
Row 20 K2tog, p, k2tog (3 sts).
Thread yarn through sts.
Darn in ends.

Stuff.
Round 16 K2tog around (6 sts).
Thread yarn through sts.
Darn in ends.

Tidy

Cast on 10 sts using any colour yarn.
Knit till strip is long enough to fit
around closed umbrella with enough
room to hold Umbrella Fellas snugly
– usually about 20cm (8in).
Cast off (bind off).

You don't have to knit the Tidy
if you don't want to, but don't
come crying to me when you
lose an Umbrella Fella. It'll be
sitting there all sad, alone and
abandoned because you couldn't
be bothered to do a little extra
knitting. Feel shame.

Remember to watch where
you're going and not get
distracted by the hypnotic
dancing of your dangling friends.
London's traffic won't stop just
because you're not looking.

FINISHING

Sew on each Fella's eyes. You can name
them too if you like.
Using black embroidery thread, sew on
the Spooks' mouths.
Hold all your Umbrella Fellas in your
cupped hands and squeeeeeee at their
overwhelming cuteness.
Sew invisible thread into the top of
each Umbrella Fella. It won't hurt them

for long. Think of it as a piercing. Tie your Umbrella Fella securely to the tip of each spine of your umbrella. Try to make sure they're facing outwards rather than looking in so they can blink endearingly at people around your umbrella.

Cover your Umbrella Fellas with waterproofing spray. Follow the instructions on the spray can.

Go outside (avoiding indoor-umbrella-opening bad luck) and open your Umbrella Fella'd masterpiece. Feel free to break out in a little project-completed celebration jig.

When you've finished dancing, attach Velcro to the two ends of the Tidy, place the Tidy around umbrella and tuck the Fellas into it to keep them safe. Sing them a nice lullaby if you want. I'm sure they'd like that.

ALL CHANGE

Umbrella Fellas are adaptable chaps. They're happy to change career at your whim. They could be earrings, pendants, charms, alternatives to corks on Australian hats, lampshade fringing, keyrings or burlesque tassels (though they may blush).

The basic shapes of the Umbrella Fellas can make many things. Sprigs can become autumn leaves in a rusty colour; Spooks turned upside down and knit in green can be juicy pears; purple Flurries with a few beads can be prim pansies; and neon-green Drips can be evil acid rain. You get the idea. Now go forth and create a few Fellas of your own devising.

The Way of **The Knit**

You are about to turn from a humble non-knitter into a crazed yarn-flinging ninja of the knit. People will stop and stand slack-jawed at your splendiferous stitching, your gorgeous garter stitch and your purling prowess. All you need to do is learn to make these little loops and Bob's your uncle, you're a real live knitter. (Your uncle doesn't have to be called Bob in order for you to be a knitter.)

> ## Abbreviations for techniques:
>
> LN – Left-hand needle
>
> RN – Right-hand needle

LIGHTS. CAMERA. CAST ON.

Casting on, making the first stitches of your project, is the opening titles to your knitting. A good cast-on sets the stage for some blockbuster knitting action and means you're well on your way to a knit you can proudly shove in the faces of other people and shout 'Look what I made!'

There are many different breeds of cast-on stitches. Some methods are better for certain projects and some are just fancy. If you want your knitting to be exactly like the pattern, use the suggested cast-on. If you're not too fussed, use your favourite cast-on and see what happens.

The slip knot

The slip knot is the start of every knitting project you'll ever make. Learn it well. The slip knot is your friend.

Follow these pictures to make your slip knot and your first cast-on stitch. Make sure you have at least a 15cm (6in) tail of yarn on your slip knot. Annoying as it might be, it is the only thing that will stop your knitting from unravelling later.

Pull the ends of the yarn to tighten your knot. Don't pull it too tight, though. You're going to have to get both your needles into that little loop in order to knit. Awwwww. Just look at it. All lonely there on the needle. It needs friends. On to the cast-on!

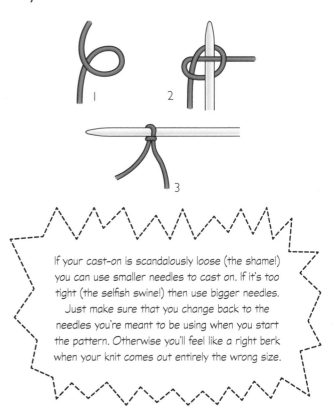

If your cast-on is scandalously loose (the shame!) you can use smaller needles to cast on. If it's too tight (the selfish swine!) then use bigger needles.
Just make sure that you change back to the needles you're meant to be using when you start the pattern. Otherwise you'll feel like a right berk when your knit comes out entirely the wrong size.

Knitted cast-on

This fairly loose cast-on uses the basic knit stitch and two needles. She's not the prettiest or neatest of cast-ons but, trust me, she is the easiest and best cast-on to start with when you're a newbie. Honest, guvnor.

1 Take two needles and make a slip knot about 15cm (6in) from the end of the yarn on one needle. Hold this needle in your left hand.

2 Insert the RN from left to right (we call this 'knitwise') into the loop on the LN. Your needles should make a cross, with your RN behind your LN. You should be able to hold both these needles with your left hand, leaving your right hand free to wrangle the yarn.

3 Wrap the yarn around and under the tip of the RN (anti-clockwise from back to front). It should end up between your RN and LN.

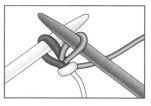

4 Slide the RN down, catch the wrapped yarn with your needle tip and pull it out of the front of the loop. You should end up with a loop on your RN.

5 Pull out the new loop a bit and then slip it onto the LN by inserting the LN underneath the loop and up through the middle.

6 Remove the RN from the loop and tug the yarn to tighten it, but not too much. Tight stitches are evil to knit with. You want your stitches nice and relaxed. You will now have two stitches on the LN.

7 Repeat the above using the new 'stitch' you just made. Keep doing this until you have as many stitches as you need.

8 You've cast on. Feel free to look a bit smug.

Cable Cast-On

The cable cast-on is a good one to swoon over. He's neat and has a firm edge that is also elastic. He's perfect for a bit of rib stitch or when you're looking for a straight-line start (such as with Baby Big Ben or Tiny Tower Bridge). You can also use him to cast on stitches in the middle of a row.

Repeat steps 1–6 of the knitted cast-on.

7 Insert the RN between the two stitches on the LN and wrap the yarn around the tip in the same way as the knitted cast on. Pull the yarn back through between the two stitches and place it on the LN, as in step 5. Repeat until you have cast on enough stitches.

To cast on extra stitches mid-row, work step 7 only, working the first stitch between the next two stitches already on the LN.

Alternate Cable Cast-On

This does all the fabulous things that the cable cast-on does but makes a pingy stretchy ribbed edge, too.

For first two stitches repeat steps 1–7 of cable cast-on.

8 Insert the RN between the two stitches on the LN from back to front.

9 Wrap the yarn around the tip from left to right.

10 With the tip of the RN push the yarn back between the two stitches, pull it out and place it on the LN.

Repeat these stitches alternately (needle from front to back, then from back to front) until you have cast on enough stitches.

Thumb cast-on

This cast-on uses one needle and is the simplest and quickest way of casting on. It can be a bit baggy though, and tends to leave you with long bits of yarn between stitches when you start to knit, causing some new knitters to go into a rabbit-in-car-headlights stare. It might be best to use it once you know what you're doing.

1 Take one needle, make a slip knot about 15cm (6in) from the end of the yarn and slip it onto the needle. Hold this needle in your right hand.

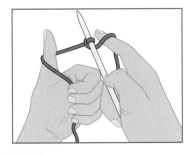

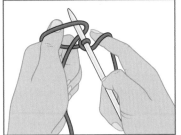

2 Wrap the yarn from the ball around your left thumb from front to back. Hold it in your palm with your other fingers.

3 Insert the needle upwards through the strand of yarn on your thumb and slip the loop into the needle.

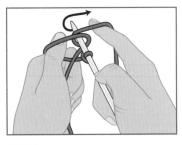

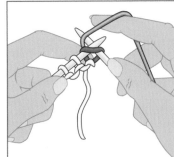

4 Pull the yarn to tighten (not too tight!) and repeat until you've cast on enough stitches.

KNIT, PURL, RULE THE WORLD

You're here at last. The moment you've been waiting for. After this you'll be a knitter. From here on in, it's a slippery slope into feeding your filthy yarn habit by selling precious family heirlooms and knitting under your desk when you're meant to be working.

Knit stitch

The best part is that if you used the knitted cast-on, you almost know how to knit already. You're going to be doing a whole lot of knit stitch, so get comfy with her. Sure, she may seem a bit confusing at first, but practise and treat her right and she'll make a nifty knitter of you. It's going to be the start of a beautiful friendship.

Start off holding the yarn at the back of the work (the side facing away from you).

1 Place the needle with the cast-on stitches in your left hand, and insert the RN into the front of the first stitch on the LN from left to right. Your needles should make a cross with your RN behind your LN. You should be able to hold both these needles with your left hand, leaving your right hand free to wrangle the yarn.

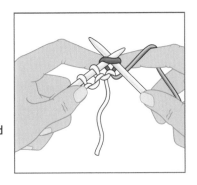

2 Wrap the yarn around and under the RN (anti-clockwise from back to front). It should end up between your RN and LN.

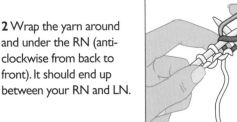

3 Slide the RN down, catch the wrapped yarn with your needle tip and pull it out of the front of the loop. You should end up with a loop on your RN.

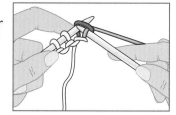

4 Slide the stitch you just looped through off the LN. Go on. Pop it off the end. You might need to shuffle the other stitches up a bit to make it easier. This has formed one knit stitch on the RN.

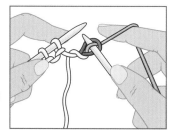

5 If it's loose, tug the yarn to tighten the stitch, but not too much. You will now have knit one stitch on the LN with the rest still on your RN.

6 Repeat the above by using the next stitch on the LN and inserting your needle in the same way. Keep doing this until all the stitches on the LN have been transferred to the RN. Yup, even that last one.

7 Sit back and admire your first knitted row. It's really rather marvellous. Allow yourself a bite of cake.

8 Now swap your needles over. Your RN becomes your LN and your LN becomes your RN. Repeat all the steps above all over again. Then again and again and again until your knitting is long enough or your arms drop off.

Important: Before you begin the next knit row, always make sure your yarn comes from the bottom of the needle to the back of the work. It must be at the back before you begin to knit. If you mysteriously get an extra stitch and your knitting is beginning to look triangular, it's because your yarn was pulled over the top of the needle. You're not prey to knitting gremlins. You just have your yarn in the wrong place.

Purl stitch

The purl stitch is a robust and manly rounded stitch. He's the reverse of the knit stitch and is a bit like knitting backwards. With the purl stitch you can make all kinds of knitting madness. He's a bit trickier than the knit stitch and some people dislike him for it. Once you get the hang of tangoing with the purl though, you're laughing. He's a reliable chap and knitting would be a sad and one-sided world without him. Once you know how to purl, you know **everything**.

Start off holding the yarn at the front of the work (the side facing you). I really, really mean it when I say HOLD IT IN FRONT. That means for **every** purl stitch. If you don't, monsters will eat you and your knitting will be in a right state, too.

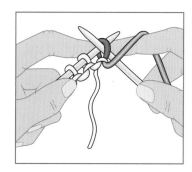

1 Place the needle with the cast-on stitches in your left hand, and insert the RN into the front of the first stitch on the LN from right to left. Your needles should make a cross, with your RN in front of your LN. You should be able to hold both these needles with your left hand, leaving your right hand free to wrangle the yarn.

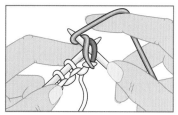

2 Wrap the yarn around and over the RN (anti-clockwise from back to front). It should end up between your RN and LN.

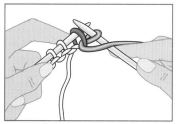

3 Slide the RN down, catch the wrapped yarn with your needle tip and push it out of the back of the loop. You should end up with a loop on your RN.

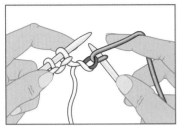

4 Slide the stitch you just looped through off the LN. Go on. Pop it off the end. You might need to shuffle the other stitches up a bit to make it easier. This has formed one purl stitch on the RN.

5 If it's loose, tug the yarn to tighten the stitch, but not too much. You will now have purled one stitch on the LN with the rest on your RN.

6 Repeat the above by using the next stitch on the LN and inserting your needle in the same way. Keep doing this until all stitches on the LN have been transferred to the RN. Yup, even that last one.

7 You purled! You're on your way to stitch sagacity.

> Learn what your stitches look like. Knit stitches resemble little Vs and purl stitches look like little bumps. An easy rhymey way to remember them is that purls curl and knits don't.

I THINK IT'S STILL MOVING! FINISH IT OFF!

So I lied about you knowing everything there was to know. You still need to learn to cast off (US: bind off). Otherwise, you'll just keep knitting and knitting, unable to stop, gradually fading away under a huge pile of endless stitches where you'll survive on cake crumbs till they can dig you out.

Casting off loops the stitches together so they can't unravel, no matter how much they might want to, and secures them to finish your project. It's a satisfying 'Byeeeee!' to your knit. Free your project from the needles!

Important: Don't cast off too tightly by pulling your yarn for all you're worth after you cast off each stitch. You'll end up with a tight and narrow end.

Cast off Knitwise

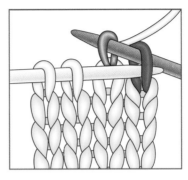

1 Knit the first two stitches. Insert the point of the LN into the front of the first stitch on the RN. You might need to tug the stitches down a bit from below to do this if your knitting is quite tight. Do it. They won't mind. They'll be too busy being excited about the cast-off.

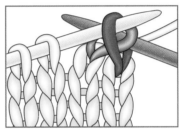

2 Lift the first stitch on the RN over the second stitch and off the needle. Be careful not to push both stitches off.

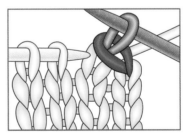

3 One stitch is left on the RN. The other is cast off. Hooray!

4 Knit the next stitch on the LN, so there are again two stitches on the RN. Lift the first stitch on the RN over the second stitch, as in step 2. Repeat this process until one stitch is left on the RN. Cut the yarn (leaving a length long enough to sew or weave in) and pass the end through the last stitch. Slip the stitch off the needle and pull the yarn end to tighten it.

Cast off purlwise

Casting off purlwise is exactly the same was casting off knitwise, just with purls instead of knits. Easy.

Cast off in pattern

If you've got a pattern in your knit – a bit of rib, a smattering of moss stitch, or something fancier – then you really should cast off in pattern to keep the edge nice and stretchy. It's not rocket science. Just knit the knit stitches and purl the purl stitches.

Ta daaah! In your sweaty paws you should now hold your very own first knitted square. Admire its beauty. Its handmade wobbly stitches and mysterious holey bits. Feel yarn-flavoured pride at your creation and fear not: you will learn to perfect your knit in time.

MORE, YOU SAY? OTHER USEFUL STITCHES AND STUFF

Garter stitch and stocking stitch

Ooh la la! Garter stitch and stocking stitch (US: stockinette stitch) are a couple of racy little numbers. They're rows of knitting that build up to form your fabric. Allow me to introduce the two main sisters of stitch patterns.

Garter stitch (g st) is made up of rows of knit knit knit knit knit knit (you get the idea). She's got wavy ridges on the front and the back, and both sides look the same. Garter stitch lies down flat and makes a thicker fabric than stocking stitch. She's the simplest stitch pattern to do. Get the hang of garter and you won't even need to look at your knitting to knit it.

Stocking stitch (st st) is made up of rows of knit then purl then knit then purl then knit (again you get the idea). She's a sleeker and neater stitch, and makes a dazzlingly lovely fabric with all the knits on one side (the right side) and all the purls on the other (the wrong side). The one thing about stocking stitch is that she never lies flat. She's a curly minx and will always roll up at the edges, no matter what you do. Stocking stitch is best for sleeves and jumpers, but is not so great for scarves.

Instructions for stocking stitch in patterns can be written like this:

Row 1 K.
Row 2 P.

Or, alternatively: Work in st st (1 row k, 1 row p), beg with a k row.

To remember which stitch sister is which, remind yourself that blushing brides normally wear one garter (just the knit stitch) and two stockings (knit and purl stitch).

Rib stitch

Rib stitch is the annoying half-brother of garter and stocking stitch. He's a mix of the two. He's the stretchy bit at the end of sleeves, collars and cuffs that keeps your ends from flapping. He's ever so satisfying to admire once you've got him right.

Rib stitch is made up of knits and purls. It can be done in any combination of numbers across a whole row; for example, rows of two knits and two purls.

Important rib stitch stuff

• The knit and purls must line up under each other. If you see a knit stitch, knit it; if you see a purl stitch, purl it.

• Pass your yarn between your needles when you change from knit to purl. This is the most important thing in the world when you are doing rib stitch. If you forget to do this, your rib stitch will be rubbish. Utter, utter rubbish. So sad.

THE WOBBLY WORLD OF INCREASING AND DECREASING

Once you get sick of squares, you'll probably want to start getting into shapes. Most newbie knitters have horror at the thought of stepping away from the comfort of plain knit and purl, but shaping is simple. You just remove or add stitches as you go. It's really easy to do, doesn't take long to learn and probably won't make you swear out loud as much as some of the more fiddly stitches you might want to learn later. Be brave and throw yourself into a bit of shaping. Go on!

Increasing Stitches

Make 1 (m1)

Make 1 (m1) magically creates a new stitch in between two existing stitches. It uses the horizontal thread that lurks between the stitches. Twisting the stitch prevents a hole appearing in your knitting and makes your increase practically invisible. I said 'practically'. There are people who will be able to see it, the eagle-eyed swines.

To twist m1 to the left

1 Work to the place you want to increase and insert the LN under the horizontal strand between the next two stitches from front to back.

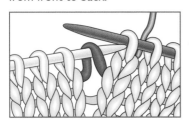

2 Knit this loop through the back to twist it.

To twist m1 to the right

1 Work to the place you want to increase and insert the LN under the horizontal strand between the next two stitches from back to front.

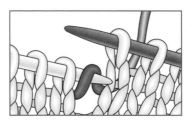

2 Knit this loop through the back to twist it.

Increase 1 (inc1)

Inc1 does what it says on the tin (increases the number of stitches by one). It is most often used at the edges of a knitted piece. Do it neatly and it's virtually invisible in the pattern of stitches. Do it badly and people will point and laugh. Try to keep an even tension as you add stitches; when you're knitting into the same stitch twice, it's easy to make it tight, and frown lines cause wrinkles in old age.

Inc1 on a knit row

1 On a knit row, knit the first stitch on the LN in the usual way, but instead of sliding the stitch off the LN as you would normally do, knit into the back of the same stitch (still keeping the yarn at the back of the work).

2 Slide the stitch off the LN. You now have two stitches on the RN and have created a stitch. Ooooh. It's like magic!

Inc1 on a purl row

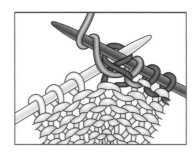

1 On a purl row, purl the first stitch on the LN in the usual way, but instead of sliding the stitch off the LN as you would normally do, purl into the back of the same stitch (still keeping the yarn at the front of the work).

2 Slide the stitch off the LN. Voila! An extra stitch.

Knit into front, back and front (kfbf)

Kfbf makes two stitches instead of one: simply knit into the front, back and then the front again of the same stitch.

Decreasing stitches

Knit two stitches together (k2tog)

The k2tog and you will get to know each other very well. It's the bog-standard method for decreasing, and it does show in the fabric as well as making it narrower.

1 Knit to where you want to decrease and insert the RN knitwise through the next two stitches on the LN.

2 Knit these two stitches together as if they were one stitch.

Purl two stitches together (p2tog)

1 Purl to where you want to decrease and insert the RN purlwise through the next two stitches on the LN.

2 Purl these two stitches together as if they were one stitch.

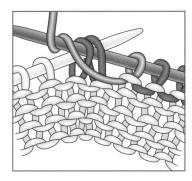

Slip two stitches (ssk), or Knit two stitches together through the back loop (k2tog tbl)

1 Slip two stitches knitwise one at a time from LN to RN (they will be twisted).

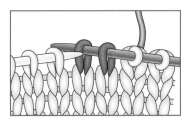

2 Insert the LN from left to right through the fronts of these two stitches and knit together as one stitch.

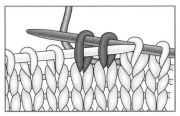

Decreasing two stitches at once

K3tog

Work as k2tog, but knit three stitches together instead of two.

P3tog

Work as p2tog, but purl three stitches together instead of two.

K3tog tbl

Work as ssk (or k2tog tbl) but slip three stitches instead of two and knit them together.

GOODBYE SEAMS, HELLO CIRCULAR KNITTING

It is a well-known fact among all knitters that sewing up seams is as close to pure evil as crafting gets. Wouldn't it be fabulous to have no seams to sew up at all? Seamless knitting is possible through the wonder that is circular knitting.

Flat knitting is knitted in rows that go back and forth and wander from one needle to the other. With circular knitting, you work round and round rather than in rows. At the end of the round, you just carry on knitting without having to swap your needles over. This makes a tube-like piece of knitting. It's the lazy knitter's dream.

Circular knitting is friend of small tubular knits like gloves, hats, socks and sleeves. It can be used for bigger things too, like laptop socks, scarves and giant man-eating pythons.

There are two ways to get your circular knit on: double-pointed needles (DPNs) or the fantastical beast that is the magic loop.

Double-pointed needles (DPNs)

Useful for self-defence in case of a zombie apocalypse, DPNs are also great for circular knitting, from teeny-tiny tubes to giant socks of doom. They're fairly easy to use, although they look more complicated than they are. They are good for using on the tube to scare people away from sitting next to you. You will generally use a set of four DPNs; three needles hold the stitches and you work with the fourth.

1 Cast on the number of stitches required on to one needle. It's best to use the knitting-on method, as the cast-on stitches need to be fairly loose.

2 You then need to divide the stitches evenly between three needles. (Note that when dividing stitches between needles, they should not be too far apart. If the stitches are stretched when the needles are joined, use a shorter needle.)

3 Make sure that the cast-on edge is facing inwards and is not twisted. If you don't do this you'll have twisted knitting. And I don't mean in the heavy metal sense.

4 Bring the three needles together to form a triangle. Place a stitch marker to indicate the end of the round (slip this on to the next needle for every round).

5 Taking your fourth needle, knit the first cast-on stitch, pulling the yarn tight to avoid creating a gap between the first and third needle.

6 Knit the remaining stitches from the first needle. The first needle is now empty and becomes the working needle.

7 Knit the stitches from the second needle onto the working needle. The second needle is now empty and becomes the working needle.

8 Knit the stitches from the third needle onto the working needle. You have now completed one round. Impressive.

9 Continue working in this way to produce a piece of tubular fabric.

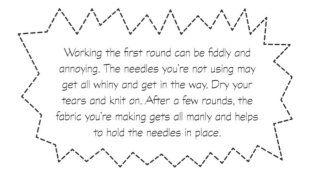

Working the first round can be fiddly and annoying. The needles you're not using may get all whiny and get in the way. Dry your tears and knit on. After a few rounds, the fabric you're making gets all manly and helps to hold the needles in place.

The magic loop

I heart magic loop more than any other knitting technique. It's not everyone's cup of tea (milk and no sugar, please), but once you and magic loop are one, nothing can stop you. You're invincible. (Please don't test this out by jumping off anything.)

Magic loop lets you use the marvel that is a circular needle (two needles joined by a thin cord) to knit any sized tube at all. Literally any size. We're talking so small you have to squint to see it. My, how I love magic loop.

1 Using a long circular needle (100cm/40in is probably best), cast on the number of stitches you need.

2 Slide them to the cable part of the circular needle.

3 Count to the halfway point in your total number of stitches and pull a section of cable out between the stitches. It doesn't need to be exactly half if the number of stitches isn't even.

4 Slide the divided stitches back up the needles.

5 Pull the RN through so half the stitches are on the cable and your RN is free to move where it pleases.

6 Join the stitches to form a ring by knitting the first half of the stitches from the LN onto the RN. You should end up with stitches on both needles again. Make sure your stitches aren't twisted before you do this.

7 Pull the cable to slide the second half of the stitches onto the LN and pull the RN through so half the stitches are on the cable. Your RN is free again.

8 Knit the second half of the stitches.

9 Repeat steps 7 to 8 for each row.

> Magic loop works best if you make sure you pull the first stitch quite tight. You'll end up with ladders otherwise. Tiny people will be able to climb up your knitting and steal stuff.

ZUT ALORS! CONTINENTAL KNITTING!

Continental knitting is often faster, involves fewer elbows flying about, and looks really cool. The main difference is that you hold your yarn in your left hand instead of your right, while the needle scoops the yarn as it goes with a flick of the finger. Some people prefer continental knitting to the usual knit. It's worth a go just to boast to people about being multi-knitual.

Continental Knit

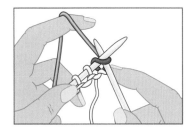

1 Hold the needle with the cast-on stitches in your left hand and the yarn over your left index finger. Insert the RN into the front of the stitch from left to right.

2 Move the RN down and across the back of the yarn.

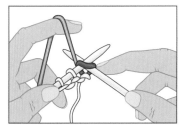

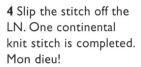

3 Pull the new loop on the RN through the stitch on the LN, using the right index finger to hold the new loop if needed.

4 Slip the stitch off the LN. One continental knit stitch is completed. Mon dieu!

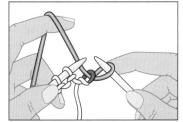

Continental purl

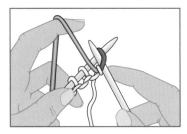

1 Hold your yarn in front of the work. In front, I say!

2 Hold the needle with the cast-on stitches in your left hand and insert the RN into the front of the stitch from right to left, keeping the yarn at the front of the work.

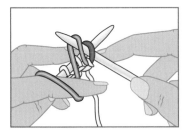

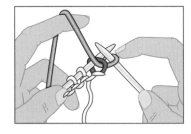

3 Move the RN from right to left behind the yarn and then from left to right in front of the yarn. Pull your left index finger down in front of the work to keep the yarn taut.

4 Pull the new loop on the RN through the stitch on the LN, using your right index finger to hold the new loop if needed.

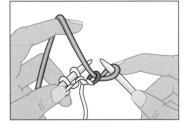

5 Slip the stitch off the LN. Return the left index finger to its position above the needle. One continental purl stitch is completed. Sacré bleu!

I CORD. YOU CORD. WE ALL CORD I-CORD.

The 'I' in I-cord stands for 'idiot'. It's called Idiot-cord because it's so easy to make that even the most feeble-minded fibre-flinger can rustle some up. I-cord can be used for all kinds of things from decorating a lovely bit o' knitting to using as a lasso to capture those winged machete monkeys that keep attacking you on the way to the Emerald City.

1 On a circular or double-pointed needle, cast on a small number of stitches. Fewer than five works best.

2 Push the stitches to the other end of the needle and turn the needle, so the first stitch you'll knit is the first one you cast on.

3 Knit the stitches, making sure you pull the yarn tight for the first stitch.

4 Shove the stitches to the other end of the needle.

5 Repeat steps 3 and 4 until the I-cord is the desired length.

6 Balance I-cord on top lip and pretend you have a droopy moustache. We've all done it.

THE BORING HORROR OF GAUGE SWATCHES

Do you want your knit to be just like the pattern in shape and size like an eerie knitted clone? I'm sorry to report that you're going to have to switch on your brain and do some maths. Sorry about that. Ladies and gents, meet the gauge swatch. He's boring. I mean, really boring. Not only do you have to do maths, but you're going to have to knit a square and find a tape measure.

If gauge is important to your knit (such as with patterns like Bag Bovver, where you need your knit the right size to fit a certain space) then you are going to have to knit a gauge square. Oh the horror! You can't even get someone else to knit it for you. Agh!

Gauge is the number of stitches and rows you have in a certain area. Almost every pattern you'll bump into will have gauge lurking somewhere near the start. Gauge instructions will look like this:
X stitches and Y rows = 10cm (4in)

Measuring gauge

You'll need to knit a square, in the same stitch pattern as the pattern you're about to make, that is a little bigger than 10 by 10cm (4 by 4in). At this point, some people cheat and knit 6 by 6cm (2½ by 2½in). But the rules tell you to do the 10cm (4in) square. Up to you if you want to break them. Just don't come crying to me from the depths of your gargantuan jumper.

1 Cast on the correct number of stitches to make 12cm (4¾in).

2 Knit till the square measures about 12cm (4¾in).

3 Block your square (wet it, pin flat without stretching, let it dry).

4 Measure your stitch count by counting how many stitches there are in 10cm (4in).

5 Measure your row count by counting how many stitches there are in 10cm (4in).

6 Check that your gauge matches up to the gauge of your pattern.

Aaaiiiieeeee! My gauge doesn't match!

Pull yourself together! It can happen to us all. No two knitters knit the same. Not even identical twins. It's been tested. Though not with clones. I'll get back to you on that after more time in the laboratory.

• If your gauge has more stitches than the pattern says, try again using bigger needles.

• If your gauge has fewer stitches than the pattern says, try again with smaller needles.

• If your gauge matches exactly, then you are truly blessed. Hail the yarn gods.

IT'S NOT ALL ABOUT KNITTING

Oi! Where do you think you're going? Now you've learnt to knit your training isn't over. There are some skills that are to knitting what mash and gravy are to meat pies. Alone they're great, but together they're fantabulous. If you keep on learning, you may one day turn yourself into a many-skilled and much-revered Swiss Army Knife of craft. So here are a couple of other useful techniques with which to make your stitching splendiferous. This is going to be the start of a beautiful fibre friendship, I can tell.

Captain Hook

Crochet! The easy-peasy technique of making a crochet chain will save you the fiddlyness of knitting a chain. It's quicker, it's less hassle and you get to wave a hook around.

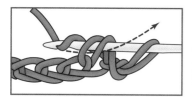

1 Make a slip knot about 6in (15cm) from the end of the yarn and put it on your hook. Hold your hook in your right hand.

2 Hold the knot between your thumb and middle finger of your left hand.

3 Put the yarn over your index finger of your left hand and hold it against your palm with your last two fingers to keep the yarn taut.

4 Wrap the yarn over the hook from back to front between the hook end and the knot.

5 Pull the yarn through the loop using the hook.

6 Repeat steps 4 and 5 until you chain is the length you want.

Pompom Perfecting

1 Cut two cardboard doughnuts. The size of these circles will depend on the size you want your pompom. The diameter (width) of the hole depends on how packed you would like your pompom to be – the larger the hole's diameter, the fuller the pompom. For an average pompom, the centre hole is approximately one-third of the circle's diameter.

2 Hold the two cardboard doughnuts together.

3 Wrap the yarn evenly around the doughnuts wrapping it from the outside through the middle and round again, working around the cardboard. Keep on doing this till the whole doughnut is wrapped in yarn. Don't worry if your yarn runs out. Just leave the 'tail' on the outside and start with a new bit. It helps not to wrap the yarn too tightly, as it'll be harder to cut it later.

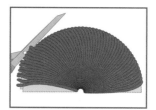

4 Once it's wrapped, use the scissors to cut along the edges of the doughnuts, a few layers of yarn at a time, until you reach the cardboard.

5 Pull the two doughnuts apart slightly. Using another piece of yarn put it between the circles and wrap it a few times along the middle. Tie it tightly.

6 Pull out the cardboard pieces.

7 Fluff up your little pompom. Trim any excess yarn. Fight the urge to put googly eyes on it and keep it as a pet.

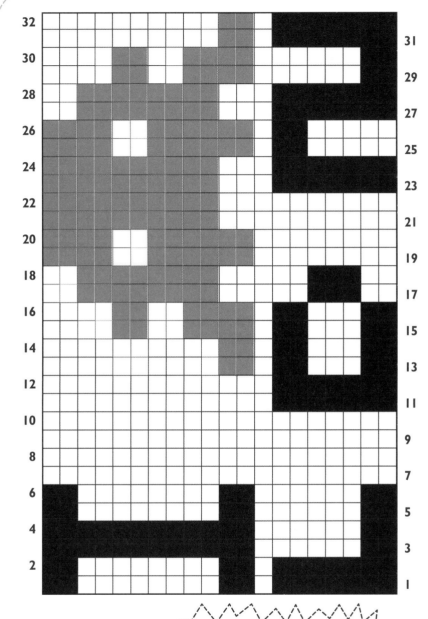

THE TELL-TALE CHART

Arrrrrrgggggghhhhhh! It's a knitting chart! Full of line upon marching line of square after square after square! And it's coming right for us! Run for the hills!

Hang on, hang on. Although a knitting chart may not look familiar, it's really very friendly. You just have to learn to understand its alien language. Here's how to translate a grid into a knitting pattern.

Why is it so hideously different?

Knitting charts are an easy way of giving a whole pile of instructions without having to write out every single one. They can be used for colourwork (multi-coloured) knitting or for fancy lace or cable patterns.

So how do I read a chart?

To read a chart, you start at the bottom right corner when you are on a knit row (or with the right side of the work facing you). When you get to the next row you're going back the other way, so read the chart from left to right. Keep going from right to left, left to right, right to left, working your way from the bottom to the top of the chart. When you reach the top you'll know it, as you'll run out of chart. Then carry on as per the rest of the pattern.

Can I make my own chart?

Why not? Just grab some grid paper and fill in your own squares. Each square is one stitch. Just remember that your stitches may be a different size from the squares on your grid so won't come out exactly as your drawing unless you do a test square and measure first.

Please note: If you're making the Space Invader Laptop Sock you will need to knit the Laptop Sock flat (rather than in the round). See instructions in 'All Change' in the pattern pages.

If you get confused, grab a trusty pencil and scribble K and P onto your chart next to each row. It's also handy to mark off the rows as you go.

Suppliers/Acknowledgments

Buttons

Daisy Moon Designs (www.daisymoondesigns.co.uk)
Wooden clock face buttons on Baby Big Ben; skull and bones buttons on Pirate Hack Sock Laptop Sock; bone buttons on Dog and Bone Mug Hugger; pig buttons on Rabbit and Pork Mug Hugger

Dress It Up Buttons (www.dressitup.com)
Buttons on Cat and Mouse, Bees and Honey and Frog and Toad Mug Huggers

Toft Buttons (www.emmatoft.co.uk)
Handmade dotty buttons on Luv a Duck Flypast Bag Bovver

All other buttons bought at Button Queen (www.thebuttonqueen.co.uk) or from eBay.

Yarns

Tubeline Scarf
Sublime Yarns (www.sublimeyarns.com); Debbie Bliss Yarns (www.debbieblissonline.com)
Thanks to Susan at Loop, Islington (www.loopknitting.com) for helping me source the yarn.

District Line green = Sublime Baby Cashmere Merino Silk DK in Froggie; Circle Line yellow = Sublime Baby Cashmere Merino Silk DK in Pineapple; Northern Line black = Sublime Merino Wool DK in Black; Waterloo and City Line turquoise = Sublime Baby Cashmere Merino Silk DK in Seesaw; Metropolitan Line magenta = Debbie Bliss Cashmerino DK in Magenta; Hammersmith and City Line pink = Sublime Baby Cashmere Merino Silk DK in Piglet; Jubilee Line grey/silver = Sublime Merino Wool DK in Grey; Central Line red = Sublime Baby Cashmere Merino Silk DK in Teddy Red; Piccadilly Line dark blue = Debbie Bliss Prima in Navy; Overground orange = Sublime Baby Cashmere Merino Silk DK in Carrots; Victoria Line light blue = Sublime Baby Cashmere Merino Silk DK in Lido; Bakerloo Line brown = Debbie Bliss Prima in Brown

Bag Bovver, Mug Huggers, Laptop Socks and Commuter Book Cosies
Cygnet Yarns Ltd (www.cygnetyarns.com)

Bag Bovver
Flying the Flag = Cygnet Acrylic DK in Red, White and Royal; Hyde Park Hive = Cygnet Acrylic DK in Bright Lime; Purly Queen = Cygnet Acrylic DK in Black; Badly Drawn Bus = Cygnet Acrylic DK in Red

Laptop Sock
Pirate Hack Sock = Cygnet Acrylic DK in Red, White and Black; Invader LDN Sock = Cygnet Acrylic DK in Light Blue, Red and Black

Mug Huggers
Dog and Bone = Premium Marvel Printed DK in colour 2005, Cygnet DK in Black; Frog and Toad = Fluorescent Cygnet DK in Bright Lime and Red; Bees and Honey = Cygnet DK in Sunshine and Black; Rabbit and Pork = Fluorescent Cygnet DK in Bright Pink, Cygnet DK in Black and White; Apples and Pears = Cygnet DK in Regal; Cat and Mouse = Cygnet DK White

All other Bag Bovvers, Mug Huggers, Laptop Socks and Commuter Book Cosies made from random unlabelled yarn bought on my world travels. Some from a street cart in India while being watched by a cow.

Umbrella Fellas
Texere Yarns (www.texere-yarns.co.uk); F W Bramwell Co & Ltd (www.bramwellcrafts.co.uk)

Drips = Bramwell 4-ply Fine Acrylic in Scarlet; Flurries and Spooks = Bramwell 4-ply Fine Acrylic in White; Sprigs = Bramwell 4-ply Fine Acrylic in Mint

All other yarn is random unlabelled yarn from my stash. It's huge and mysterious.

Acknowledgments

Huge woolly hugs to: Katy, Ali and Jennifer, my many-headed commissioning editor. Especially Katy for being so patient in the face of me trying to fit a book into the woolly whirlwind of my life. Mia for her kick-ass design work; Marilyn, Nicola and Jeni for managing to edit and create a book around my 'interesting' style of writing; Sian and Jack for making my crazed idea of having London as 'the model' come to life in the bitter city cold. The brilliant Carol, my 'floats like a butterfly, stings like a bee' agent, who keeps making me an author despite my doubts. My marvellous mum, the night-stitching Madame Molet, who I will no doubt ask to knit till 4 a.m. many times in my life and will always stay up till 5 a.m. to make sure it's perfect. Mole, Max, Neh, Judy and all five of the cats for occasionally disturbing responses to 'What do you think of this idea?' Ellen and Sarah, my fellow Fleece Stationers, for emergency tangerines, already peeled, much-needed cheerleading, and impressive modelling finesse. Amy for mini-me wig genius; Perri for kindly shoving D&C in my direction, and Emma for brilliant buttons and craft wisdom that I will always envy. Not forgetting Julia Goolia, my cheerleader down under. The good people of Twitter for virtual cake and squid-based pick-me-ups. The good people of Stitch London for actual cake and squid-based pick-me-ups, especially Linda, Laptop Sock knitter extraordinaire. And, as ever, extra woolly hugs to my long-suffering Sheepsketcher for bearing my descent into knitted madness with patience, pep talks, endless supplies of instant noodles and terrible, terrible puns.

Knitters

Tubeline Scarf knitter and part Telephone Box embroiderer: Brigitte 'Madame Molet' Onyskiw

Pirate and Space Invader Laptop Sock knitter: Linda Laidlaw Plarn square knitters: Amy 'Gerty's Rage Counsellor' Shannon, Clare Tovey, Emma Toft, Dawn Bray, Linda Laidlaw, Jo Molloy, Toria Standfield, Hannah Wilson, Annette Atkins, Adriana Medina, Ranveig Svenning Berg, Rachel Taylor, Jane Gois, Martina Povolna, Maddie Emberton, Beryl Scott, Eva Di Franco, Helen Hughes, Angela Garland, Lucy McAnish, Salima Hirani, Haroun Daley, Sophie Allott, Helen Shipley, Laura Whitaker, Annabelle Letford, Virginia Risso, Shazia Kay, Babs Taylor, Catherine Walter, Clare Chapman, Maria-Jesus Rojo, Maria Rojo, Rowan Brown, Claire Murray, Aoife Doyle and Jenny Willett.

All other knits: Lauren 'Deadly Knitshade is tired can she stop knitting now?' O'Farrell.

About the Author

Writer, traveller and giant squid wrestler, Lauren O'Farrell runs Stitch London, the UK's woolly Godzilla of a knitting community, as Head Woolly Godzilla Wrangler (official title). She is also rumoured to be sneaky stitching graffiti knitter Deadly Knitshade, of Knit the City fame, though she will neither confirm nor deny this if you ask. She lives in London with five cats and Plarchie, an 8-metre knitted squid. She works from the Fleece Station studio in Deptford.

More about Lauren... www.whodunnknit.com
Join Stitch London... www.stitchLDN.com